MW00388391

FILL A NEED

FILL A NEED

13

CRITICAL TIPS FOR SUCCESS IN BUSINESS AND LIFE

BRENT W. WARNOCK

Hegemony Press
An imprint of Cedar Fort, Inc.
Springville, Utah

© 2011 Brent Warnock
All rights reserved.

No part of this book may be reproduced in any form whatsoever, whether by graphic, visual, electronic, film, microfilm, tape recording, or any other means, without prior written permission of the publisher, except in the case of brief passages embodied in critical reviews and articles.

The views expressed within this work are the sole responsibility of the author and do not necessarily reflect the position of Cedar Fort, Inc., or any other entity.

ISBN 13: 978-1-59955-954-4

Published by Hegemony Press, an imprint of Cedar Fort, Inc., 2373 W. 700 S., Springville, UT 84663
Distributed by Cedar Fort, Inc., www.cedarfort.com

LIBRARY OF CONGRESS CATALOGING-IN-PUBLICATION DATA

Warnock, Brent, 1966- author.
 Fill a need : 13 critical tips for success in business and life / Brent Warnock.
      pages cm
 Includes bibliographical references and index.
 ISBN 978-1-59955-954-4 (alk. paper)
 1. Success in business. 2. Success. I. Title.

 HF5386.W244 2011
 650.1--dc23

2011032556

Cover design by Brian Halley
Cover design © 2011 by Lyle Mortimer
Edited and typeset by Kelley Konzak

Printed in the United States of America

10 9 8 7 6 5 4 3 2 1

Printed on acid-free paper

I dedicate this work to those who have taught
me the most important lessons of all:
my three children.

PRAISE FOR *FILL A NEED*

"Anyone who seriously desires to build and maintain a successful business needs to embrace the wisdom contained in this book's 13 tips."

Wayne Giles
Giles Disability Law

"This informative book [is] an easy read. It offers excellent business advice and experienced insight for anyone who owns a small business or is considering a small business start-up."

Dennis G. Heiner
Former Exec. Vice President
and Group President
Black & Decker Co.

"Brent speaks with authenticity, as he has navigated the difficult trenches of entrepreneurship challenges and has overcome those challenges to build successful businesses."

Blair K. Carruth, PhD
Dean, School of Business
Salt Lake Community College

"*Fill a Need* offers simple, practical, and proven success tips that I have employed successfully in my own business endeavors."

Jens Bach Nielsen
Owner
pictureline/pictureline.com

CONTENTS

FOREWORD

LIFE AND BUSINESS ARE dangerous. There are rapids, boulders, sink-holes, and dangers on every side. Obstacles on the water, in the water, and on the shore must be avoided. But once you become aware of the dangers and understand the secrets of successful passage, ultimate joy, excitement, and exhilaration await you. This book provides you with words of experience from one adventurer who has journeyed the rapids of business life and who has tasted the fruits of success.

You will find this book inherently different than most. Life's greatest lessons are often learned from failures rather than successes. Stories of mistakes and failures, however, are consistently hidden, forgotten, or purposely omitted from books intent on detailing successes. When hearing stories of success, I find it worthwhile to always ask: what failures preceded success?

Literally, it has taken thirty-plus years and over $1 million to produce this book. The stories that are shared herein are costly lessons learned. In a very real sense, this book could be considered a business survival guide. Survival guides, by nature, are lessons that can literally keep you alive by sharing the trials and errors experienced by those who have gone before. This is that kind of book. If you adhere to the survival tips discussed herein, you can save hundreds of thousands of dollars—and hours—in your future business adventures.

This book outlines what I believe are the 13 most critical lessons necessary for success in business and life. Each of these

Success Tips is a lesson learned as a result of mistakes, errors in judgment, and costly failures. I share these stories openly in hopes that you will avoid the perils and leap more directly to success.

I salute you as one willing to learn from others. Experience is a great teacher—but wiser still are those who are humble enough to learn from the experiences of others.

INTRODUCTION

Retire by Age Forty

Since I was a child, I had a goal to retire by the time I was forty years old. I am not exactly sure where this insatiable desire originated, but possibly, it came from watching my father leave for work every morning, extremely frustrated. Perhaps my yearning also originated from watching him return home at night even more frustrated than when he left. Possibly it came from overhearing my parents, neighbors, and friends' parents discuss their own horrific experiences of working forty-plus hours a week.

I clearly remember overhearing many conversations of complaint, concern, frustration, and resignation, focused on the horrors of working for someone else. Yet I remember just as clearly how the atmosphere would immediately change when the conversations would shift from the horrors of work to the joys of eventual retirement. These dialogues always began with the same statement: "When I retire I will . . ."

Regardless of the specific dreams and wishes that finished that sentence, I felt the feelings and emotions surrounding the dialogue. A magical feeling entered into the room that even a child could detect. It was as if the adults involved in the conversation allowed themselves to breathe freely—for the first time in a long time. There was a relaxing tone. There was a calming demeanor. There was laughter. There was passion. There was positive energy. There was happiness. There was peace. There was joy.

In these conversations about future retirement, I would often hear the phrases "finally," "at last," and "imagine when I am able to do what I want to do." I suppose my insatiable desire to retire early was rooted in childhood. If retirement was where happiness was to be found, I wanted to experience it early—and sooner rather than later.

In retrospect, I find it humorous that as a five-year-old I would think such thoughts. I was not in kindergarten yet and was busy planning an early retirement. Nevertheless, I had made up my mind. I was going to retire early. I was going to retire by the time I was forty—period! Moreover, I did!

The Promise—Thirty Years in the Making

- Do you find yourself dreaming of the day when you can retire?
- Do you find yourself silently wishing for the day that financial concerns, economic worries, and difficult work relationships were gone, forever?
- Do you find yourself envious of those who seem to have the perfect life; a great career, fine cars, beautiful homes, vacation escapes, and an apparent lack of concern about money in general?

If so, this book is for you. Obviously, I cannot promise you that by simply reading a book all your dreams will come true. I cannot promise that all your financial, economic, and social worries will be magically resolved. Yet, I can make you this promise: I promise this book will bring you real hope. Further, I promise that this book will provide you with real, practical, proven, and doable strategies that will set you on the path toward the life that you have imagined.

You may be asking yourself, "How can he make such a promise?"

Fill a Need was written with the intent that it will provide you, the reader, with many Success Tips that, if adhered to, will lead to success in both business and life. Notice I did not say "may" or "can"—I said they *will* lead to success.

Over the course of thirty years, I have been involved in dozens of new business start-ups. Over this time, I have made some great business decisions. I have also made some very poor decisions. I have made many gains and suffered some significant losses. I have been run over by more than one bus (figuratively speaking) only to get up, brush myself off, and keep going. I have had many sleepless nights and stressful days. However, in the end, I have done what I loved, enjoyed most of it, and, for the most part, been successful.

Through many experiences, I have learned many invaluable lessons on what it takes to be successful in business and life. The 13 secrets I share in this book are a result of lessons learned. You could call them the "checklist for success." Before engaging in any new business adventure, I personally ensure that I adhere to this checklist.

I share the checklist with you in hopes that you will avoid some of the pain—and experience more of the pleasure—that a successful business provides. You will find this book inherently different than many books touting successful and proven strategies for business. I believe that most of the greatest lessons learned are not a result of one's successes, but rather from one's failures. Hence, you will discover within these pages many honest stories of hard lessons learned while running the rapids of business life. It is not easy to openly share errors in judgment, mistakes made, and costly business failures, yet, in looking back over my thirty-plus years of business experiences, it is precisely the lessons I learned from failures that lead to eventual success.

You are most likely reading this because you also have an interest in business. Possibly, you are already knee-deep in your own business. Maybe you are pondering taking the plunge. Perhaps you are merely flirting with the idea of leaving the safety of employment shores to begin your own enterprise. Perhaps you have absolutely no intention of starting your own business but the title *Fill a Need: 13 Critical Tips for Success in Business and Life* caught your attention. Or perhaps you are a professional student, always learning, always seeking, and always reading but, for a multitude of reasons, you have never taken a plunge into entrepreneurial waters.

Regardless of your reason for reading this book, I salute you as one willing to learn from others. Had I had the foresight to pick up a book like this years ago, I would be much farther ahead than I am now. Experience is a great teacher—but wiser still are those who are humble enough to learn from the experience of others.

A River Runs Through It

One of my favorite movies is Robert Redford's 1992 classic, *A River Runs Through It*. While attending graduate school at the University of Utah, my mentor, Dr. Rogers, showed this movie in class. We analyzed a host of movies that semester, but *A River Runs Through It* caught my attention like no other.

Though I would enjoy providing an in-depth, detailed analysis of many parts of this film, it is most appropriate to mention only the final scene of the movie. *A River Runs Through It* is a movie about early life in rural Montana. Although the narrative is a fictional account of a boy named Norman, his brother Paul, and their life experiences growing up in Montana, it could be a movie of everyone's life choices. Consider the final words of the film as narrated by Robert Redford himself:

> Eventually all things merge into one,
> and a river runs through it.
>
> The river was cut by the world's great flood,
> and runs over rocks from the basement of time.
>
> On some of the rocks are timeless raindrops.

Under the rocks are the words,
and some of the words are theirs.

I am haunted by waters.

Redford's inspired words illustrate how each of our lives—like raindrops—merge, eventually becoming one great river. This great river flows where others have gone before. It is, after all, the words of others (parents, grandparents, neighbors, siblings, teachers, clergy, friends, and so on) that influence not only who we are today but also who we will be tomorrow.

Fill a Need is an attempt to provide you with some words from one who has gone before. Lessons learned through experience will help you traverse a little safer through the rapids and waterfalls of business and life. The world of business, as is life, is dangerous. There are rapids. There are rocks. There are waterfalls and sinkholes on every side. There are obstacles to avoid on the water, in the water, and beneath the water, as well as on the shore.

This book is not meant to be a complete and comprehensive guide for managing your business or your life. Rather, it is purposefully positioned in a story-oriented format to assist those who follow in avoiding some of the hazards and obstacles that all entrepreneur travelers must eventually face. By applying these Success Tips, you will find yourself enjoying the many benefits of business ownership while simultaneously avoiding some of the more dangerous and costly pitfalls inherent in exciting entrepreneurial explorations.

American Idol

I have been captivated with the television reality series *American Idol* since its inception. Possibly, you too have looked on with awe at the number and quality of singers emerging from this show year after year. Dozens of artists discovered on this show have gone on to produce tremendously successful hit songs and albums. A few have become some of the most successful artists in the music industry today.

What I find most intriguing is the realization of just how talented many unknown singers truly are. Before appearing on *American Idol*, every one of these singers was literally unknown. Like you and me, they were seemingly faceless individuals, living quietly in crowds, going to school, working jobs, and hoping for more. It amazes me how talented so-called common, normal, typical, and everyday individuals really are. Popular artists like David Archuleta, David Cook, Chris Daughtry, Carrie Underwood, Jordin Sparks, Adam Lambert, and Kelly Clarkson were yesterday's unknowns.

American Idol is a show that testifies how talented and powerful most of us really are.

So, what propelled these common, normal, typical, and everyday people to stardom? Is it simply a lucky break? Being in the right place at the right time? Having a special gift? Yes, undoubtedly, many variables align to form a path to success. There is, however, one essential element that every one of these successful *American Idol* finalists has in common. They tried out. They stepped up to the plate. They plunged into the waters.

Literally, each of these contestants had to walk to the audition. Do not overestimate the simplicity of this. This was no easy task. Ask anyone who has auditioned for the show. Nearly every location that stages an *American Idol* tryout has in excess of 10,000 contestants. Imagine showing up for an audition to learn that you are number 8,588. The wait seems endless. It is hot. It is humid. If you look at it logically—honestly—what is the chance that you will be one of the finalists?

Typically, at each tryout location, only about 20 of the 10,000-plus contestants receives a "golden ticket." On the show, a golden ticket means that you are invited to go to Hollywood week. Hollywood week is an additional, week-long, intense tryout event. The odds of an invitation to Hollywood week are less than two-tenths of 1 percent (2 in every 1,000 contestants).

It makes you wonder how many attended the audition, recognized the odds, thought about the futility of the attempt, and returned home or back to work. Those who did not stay will never know. Sure, the odds were against them. They are against all of us. The odds were stacked against me when I set off to retire by the time I was forty. Nevertheless, each successful contestant took the first step. They showed up.

Action is based on belief. To show up and try requires that you believe that you can be successful. With no belief, there is no action. Maybe this is why the *American Idol* judges almost invariably ask each contestant the same question:

"Why are you here today?"

Why do you suppose that this is the first question they usually ask every contestant? If you have watched the show faithfully, you also are familiar with the typical answer: "I am here to be the next American Idol." So why do the judges ask the question if they already know the answer? The answer to this is likely found in the next question the judges typically pose:

"Do you think that you can be the next American Idol?"

American Idol viewers realize that the show is not only about finding the greatest voices. No doubt, possessing a vocal instrument and being able to sing is a necessity, but the judges are looking for much more. True artists have strong characteristics: a quality of essence and a charming charisma that goes beyond a great voice.

The judges look for more than vocal talents; they look for character talents as well. They search for those who can sing and those who believe in themselves and their talent. True artists carry themselves with confidence, with skill, but most importantly—with passion. In other words, the judges search for those who have passion. Passion is discussed in detail in this book as one of the secrets of future success, but it suffices to say here that passion is just as critical in business and life as it is for contestants on *American Idol*.

As previously mentioned, the odds of success on *American*

Idol are somewhat slim. However, as an entrepreneur, your odds of success are much better. The Small Business Administration recently revealed that two-thirds of new small businesses survive at least two years, and 44 percent survive at least four years. Approximately six hundred thousand new businesses begin each year. Do you have the desire, the belief, the confidence, and most importantly, the passion that you can be one of those six hundred thousand to start a new business this year? Better yet, ask yourself the same question the judges would ask:

"Do you think you can be a successful entrepreneur?"

Listen to your answer carefully—it may have more to do with your future than you think.

Consider one of my favorite thoughts, by anthropologist Clifford Geertz:

"We all begin with the [opportunity] to live a thousand kinds of life but end in the end having lived only one."[1]

Originally, I was introduced to this thought during my graduate studies in communication at the University of Utah. In the original quote, Geertz used the term "natural equipment" rather than "opportunity" because he was speaking of genetic selection. However, I believe the thought is more powerful when we speak of human choices and opportunity. I have taught a variety of communication courses at several nearby universities and colleges over the past fifteen years. Invariably, I introduce this thought to the students by posing the question:

"What could you have done today besides coming to class?"

The answers begin.

- I could have stayed in bed.
- I could have stayed at work.
- I could have studied for the exam I have in my next class.
- I could have stayed home and watched TV.
- I could have gone to the game, gone out to eat, gone to a movie, and so on.

While the students respond, I draw a myriad of short lines originating from a single point, visually indicating the innumerable possibilities of choosing different actions (see figure 1a).

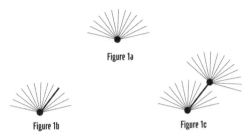

Figure 1a

Figure 1b

Figure 1c

Then I continue. "But each of you in this room *did* choose to come to class. That was a conscious choice among many competing alternatives."

I then proceed to darken one of the lines on the diagram to highlight a path chosen (see figure 1b). I go on to pose another question:

"What could you choose to do this very moment?"

Some class member inevitably responds, "I could stand up and leave."

"You are absolutely right."

I draw one line originating at the dot, representing the present moment (see figure 1c). With the understanding that indeed each one of them is completely free to leave the class, the answers now come in droves. With each answer, I detect a slight hint of excitement as they seriously consider their alternatives.

- I could leave and go watch TV.
- I could drive to Vegas.
- I could go snowboarding.
- I could go do lunch with my girlfriend.

Again, I visually represent all the potential paths of action (see figure 1d).

Figure 1d

I then ask one final question:

"What are you going to do after class?"

Again, a variation of similar answers are provided, and I illustrate each with a line.

Figure 1e

"You see, each one of us has the opportunity to live literally a thousand kinds of life, but, in the end, you can only live one in each moment. In addition, snaking through the thousands of possible paths—looking like the branches of a tree—is one highlighted path indicating what you choose to do out of all the possibilities that lie before you. Literally, *you* choose the path of *your* life." (See figure 1e.)

As you look over these visuals, it is important to note that once you make a choice and start down a particular path, you cannot turn back. The alternatives that existed at that previous moment are gone. Some options are gone forever. Actions are irreversible. You cannot undo an action. Behavior has no opposite. Sure, you can choose differently in the "now"—but you cannot change your choice in the past. Hence, decisions in the moment are incredibly powerful.

Therefore, it may be valuable to ask one final time:

"Do you think you can be a successful entrepreneur?"

For this to be a reality, you must first believe it. It must first be a choice. Then you put your belief into action. Action stems from thoughts. My only intent in this first section is to open up your mind to the possibilities. If you believe, all things can be yours.

I not only believed it was possible to retire by the time I was forty, but I also knew it would happen. I did not know the specifics, nor did I have an exact plan. I had no specific direction. I did not know the details; I just knew retiring before I was forty years old was my destiny.

If I Can Do It—You Can Do It

At this point, you may be saying "Great," "Wonderful," "Good on you," and I wouldn't be surprised if your tone of voice included a bit of sarcasm. I understand that you are not reading this book to learn about my successes. You are interested in creating your own.

Here's the point. I am not wise beyond my years. I am not more intelligent. I am not luckier. I am not from a wealthy background. In reality, being successful in business is not about me at all. Nor is it about you. Starting a successful business is about one simple action. And this simple action—if you take it to heart, if you believe it, if you dedicate your life to it—will not only ensure your success, it will also make your goal achievable, your life livable. Yes—it will make your dreams come true.

This "it" is something you can begin doing today.

- You can do "it" wherever you are.
- You can do "it" regardless of whatever else you may be doing.

- You can do "it" at home.
- You can do "it" at work.
- You can do "it" at play.
- You can do "it" at church.
- You can do "it" at a mall.
- You can do "it" at a restaurant.
- You can do "it" at a beach.
- You can do "it" on the court.
- You can do "it" at the gym.

To excel, you need to do "it" in all these places.

- "It" does not take money.
- "It" does not take intelligence.
- "It" does not take luck.
- "It" does not take education.
- "It" does not take wealth.

What is the secret?
What is the action?
What is "it"?

Note

1. Clifford Geertz, *The Interpretation of Cultures* (New York: Basic Books, 1973), 45.

SUCCESS TIP #1
WHAT IS "IT"?

A FEW YEARS AGO, I was invited to speak at a local college entrepreneurship forum. This is an annual event in which the business department invites the entire student body to participate in an afternoon of forums and seminars all centered on entrepreneurship. Each year a selection of local entrepreneurs, business owners, and scholars are invited to speak.

On this particular day, I was the second speaker, following the keynote presenter. This keynote speaker, who I did not know, caught my attention immediately. He was fashionably dressed, probably in a 2,000-dollar suit and expensive shoes. He indeed looked the part of a successful entrepreneur. I was excited to hear what he would say. He began:

"I have been asked to speak to you today about entrepreneurship. I want to focus my remarks on the single most important aspect of business ownership."

He had me intrigued. I was excited to hear the answer. The entire room fell quiet as we waited for the mystery to be revealed.

"The single most important aspect of starting a business is in how you dress," he exclaimed proudly. "Dress for Success!"

I was stunned. This was not the answer that I had anticipated. As I listened on for the next hour as he spoke of professionalism, conduct, salesmanship, and how it all begins with one's appearance, I began to question the wisdom of such claims. I looked at my own dress—business casual—which actually was a step up from my typical jeans and collared shirt. I began to worry. How will the audience receive me now that all eyes were focused on one's dress and appearance?

More importantly, I began to seriously question the value of his comments. Most of the highly successful entrepreneurs I associate with love to dress down. They enjoy working in jeans, shorts, sweats, or even pajamas. They savor the freedom of not having to conform to some externally applied dress code from some authority or employee handbook. In fact, for many entrepreneurs, it was the dress code and other formal policies that motivated them to start their own businesses. They were fed up with being told what to do, what to wear, how they should look, or how they *should* behave. As one of my associates was fond of saying: "Don't should on me and I won't should on you."

Soon the keynote speaker concluded and the master of ceremonies introduced me. Being somewhat concerned with the previous speaker's comments, I quickly altered my prepared remarks and began by saying:

"This is the beauty of being asked to contribute in a setting like this—we each can offer what we feel is the basic, essential, most important ingredient required for successfully starting and running a business."

I then drew nine underlines on the board that looked like this:

$$\underline{\quad}\ \underline{\quad}\ \underline{\quad}\ \underline{\quad}\ \ \underline{\quad}\ \ \underline{\quad}\ \underline{\quad}\ \underline{\quad}\ \underline{\quad}!$$

It was a hangman game.

"This is what I feel is the most important element of starting and running a business."

I now had the audience's attention. I waited and allowed them time to ponder and question, and finally they began to play. "Give me an A," someone from the back shouted. I complied and placed an A above the middle line. Slowly, as they shouted out vowels and consonants, the puzzle was completed.

F I L L   A   N E E D !

This book is a result of that successful presentation. The entrepreneurship forum for that year became known as the forum that "filled a need." This principle seemed to weave itself through most of the conversations, questions, and breakout sessions for the remainder of the day. In closing, the master of ceremonies stated that the forum itself had "filled the needs" of all the attendees as envisioned by the business department.

Indeed, filling a need is the "it."

- "It" is what business is about.
- "It" is the key to success.
- "It" is learnable.
- "It" is exercisable.
- "It" is obtainable.
- "It" will make your dreams come true.
- "It" is the most important and basic element necessary for any successful enterprise.

It is important to identify here what "it"—filling a need—is not.

- "It" is not about you.
- "It" is not about me.
- "It" is not about ego.
- "It" is not about money.
- "It" is not about intellect.
- "It" is not about connections.
- "It" is not about political power.

Rather:

- "It" is about others.
- "It" is that simple.

Let us explore "it"—filling a need—a little more in depth.

If you can fill a need, you can successfully own, manage, and run your own business.

Anyone who has ever started a successful business has undoubtedly noticed, identified, and filled a need of someone else, regardless of whether the need they filled was filled by a product or a service. Regardless of whether the need they filled was for one customer or a group of consumers. In order to start a business, you must find a need and fill it. It is that simple. Without filling a need, there would be no business, no product, no service, and no customers. You can operate a business in your pajamas quite successfully. You can wear sweats and still run a successful enterprise. However, without filling a need, you have no business.

Consider a few quick examples:

Ben & Jerry's Ice Cream

Ben and Jerry did not invent ice cream. Ice cream has been around for thousands of years. However, Ben and Jerry did notice, identify, and fill a need for new and unique flavors of high quality ice cream.

Wrigley filled a need with chewing gum.

Google fills a need.

eBay fills a need.

Heinz fills a need.

Microsoft fills a need.

Obviously, I could continue to name every major and minor, large and small business operating on the planet today, and every one of them fills a consumer need.

Every successful business has proceeded along a continuum of noticing, identifying, and then filling needs. In addition, every successful company that remains in business continues along this continuum of filling needs today or they simply would not exist.

You may be tempted to dismiss these claims as being too simplistic, too easy, or too vague. In response, I can say only that I attribute my own success in business to this simple idea. But hang on. There is more to filling a need than meets the eye.

Identifying a Need

At this point, you may be asking the most elementary of questions. "If starting a business is as simple as identifying and filling a need, why have I not started a business yet?" Good question. Identifying a need starts a lot more basic than what you may be thinking. Most importantly, filling a need is a skill that you can begin to exercise and strengthen starting today.

Begin Exercising Today

It may be helpful to think of the process of filling a need as a muscle. It is a muscle that you can exercise just like any other. It needs warming up. It needs practice. It needs stretching. Noticing and then filling a need is a habit that you form. Filling a need is a way of being; it literally becomes who you are. Filling a need requires that you really begin seeing the world around you. When you see the world from a "needs" perspective, it's as if you put on a different set of eyeglasses. The world becomes new to you for you begin to realize that only you can see the world from your vantage point. Seeing the way you do is something unique that only you can do. You are the only one standing in your position, seeing the world from your vantage point, from your perspective, with your eyes.

Try the following interesting and revealing exercise. Watch how rarely the people around you truly notice others in need. When you walk out of your home, office, gym, church, or classes today, observe others closely. Notice how few people are aware of the world around them. If you do not believe me, perform this simple experiment. Load yourself up with a laptop, a box of books, two bags, and a backpack. Now proceed to the nearest exit door where there are bound to be numerous people. Walk through the door and note how many people truly recognize your need? How many hold the door open? How many let you go first? How many offer to help? How many notice your dilemma? It may surprise you.

Though there are those who do notice others' needs, unfortunately they are not in the majority. Do not get me wrong. I know that most people are inherently good. We are willing to help others when we notice that help is needed. The problem arises from *not* noticing that help is needed.

I had such an experience the other day. I was leaving my college class and was loaded down with a laptop, a projector, a couple of books, and a backpack. Packed classes were dismissed, and the hallways quickly filled with students eager to get away. The exit door was approaching quickly and surely, and with this many students exiting at the same time, I thought I would have no problem with the doors. As I neared the exit, a number of students who were walking directly in front of me hit the door open, walked through, and then, as if they had no idea anyone was behind them, allowed the door to slam closed in my face. Luckily I managed to get a foot between the door and the frame, and with great difficulty I struggled to twist, flip, and kick the door open just enough for me to proceed through. All the while, I noticed how students continued to file out of the building, simply choosing to go around me and exit through adjoining doors. *How rude!* I thought initially. Then as I walked with the sea of students and observed the ant-like crawls of a crowd of escaping students, it hit me—these students were not intending to be rude or callused in their behavior; they were simply unaware.

Many of us walk around on this planet not fully aware of others. We are preoccupied. We have our own schedules, our own tasks, our own appointments, our own problems, our own issues, and our own lives. It is often an exhausting task simply trying to balance the details of our own lives, our problems, our finances, our relationships, our worries, and our concerns. How can we be concerned with filling the needs of others when our own loads are heavy to bear? The answer is ironic. The best way to ensure that you and your family are cared for is to lose yourself in the service of others. In other words—and it is paradoxical—as you begin to notice, identify, and fill the needs of others, your own needs will be filled as well.

Who Needs?

Discovering and distinguishing personal needs is not difficult. For example, pay attention as you drive today. Is there a car that is signaling to merge into your lane? They have a need. You can fill it. *Let them in.* Is there a pedestrian standing at the crosswalk waiting for the traffic to slow? They have a need. You can fill it. Stop and wave them across. As you move about at work, school, stores, banks, fitness centers, golf courses, ball fields, stadiums, and streets, pay attention to those around you. This is how you can begin to exercise your fill a need muscle. Who needs a door opened? Who needs a smile? Who needs a call? Who needs a word of encouragement? Who needs a pat on the back? Who needs a tip? Who needs a handout? Who needs training? Who needs a little kindness? Begin today by taking advantage of all the needs that exist around you.

We live in a world of needs. Needs are everywhere. Every person on the planet has needs. Everyone who crosses your path, who walks your way, who drives alongside you—they all have needs. Your first step is simple: pay attention. Begin today to exercise your notice of needs muscle. This is the first step in building your own business. It is important that you begin training yourself to really see the needs of others. The world provides. There are needs all around. Once you start paying attention, you will be amazed at how many needs there are on all sides. Needs that need to be filled. Needs that you can fill.

Western Economic Culture

Ironically, our western economic culture focuses us inward. The hard-driving economic machinery of our present culture is all about the attainment of money. It is all about taking care of "me." It is pushing ahead. It is making the sale. It is a culture of me-ism. Rather than look out for others, our individualistic society seems to demand that we care only for ourselves. After all, we are often taught, if you do not watch out for yourself, who will?

The irony is that only when you help others are you capable of helping yourself. Every employment position you have ever held was created by a need. You were paid only because you were able to fill someone else's need. Business ownership is no different. Only by servicing someone's needs are you able to make a sale. Therefore, though our culture is inherently selfish, ironically our heritage's foundation is one of service to others. Our economic engine is about others. In the end you receive only when you give, obtain only when you help, acquire only when you serve, and thrive only when you provide. Those who recognize and understand this paradox are those who succeed financially.

Peeking into Other Worlds

The power of forcing yourself to look outside of yourself and into the lives of others enables you to peek into other worlds. You have lived in your world a long time. Out of habit, you are most likely looking over the most crucial needs of those closest to you. It is natural for us to become so accustomed to a situation that we simply do not see the obvious. It may be difficult to truly realize what needs need filling—especially of those closest to you (spouse, children, siblings, parents, and neighbors).

Tree Literacy

We recently had our yard landscaped. Rather than build a fence separating us from the neighbors, we wanted to leave it open yet create some semblance of privacy. Our landscaper suggested trees. Over the course of the summer, we planted sixty or more trees. Through this process, I have become tree literate, a tree guru. I now recognize trees. I know their leaves, their names, their expected dimensions and proper placements. Now when I drive through neighborhoods or walk down streets, I find myself noticing particular trees in the neighborhood. Trees I had never noticed. Having learned something about the characteristics of trees, I can intelligently analyze landscaping in a completely new way. I constantly find myself reviewing whether a particular tree is positioned wisely, whether it was used appropriately in the space, and so on. I am amazed at the new world that has opened for me in learning about trees.

Need Literacy

Filling a need is no different from recognizing trees. There is a new world you can experience if you will only open your eyes. Ask yourself, what does my neighbor need? What do they lack? Begin to pay attention, watch, talk to others, observe. Ask.

What could be wrong with asking our neighbor directly, "Do you need anything?" or "How may I help?" "What problems are you facing?" "What help do you need?" I believe we often are afraid to ask because they might actually make a suggestion.

If you find yourself fearful of what may be required of you if you truly begin to notice others' needs, you are getting the point. This fear is exactly what has hindered you from discovering dozens of hidden business ideas that have always existed in your world. The objective is to open up your eyes to this new world. Allow yourself to see the world differently than you have seen it before.

In order to see beyond what you have always seen in your world, you must place yourself in a discover-the-needs-of-others mind-set. As with any new skill, the ability to see differently comes first through education (the purpose of this book) and then through practice. Do not forget that whether or not you choose to actually fill an observed need is up to you. I would emphasize, however, that there is a reason this section was titled "Fill a Need" rather than "Observing" or "Noticing a Need." The actual proactive practice of filling an observed need is a central part of the process of learning how to fulfill the needs of others.

Unique Needs

There is a subtle yet vibrant power in suggesting you look around your world and notice the needs of those near you. You are absolutely unique. You live in a particular city. You live at a particular time. You live on a particular street. You have a unique social circle. You belong to a unique family. You have unique friends and neighbors. You experience a world that no one else on the planet is experiencing. Your job, your school, your church, your stores, and your streets all create a unique tapestry of people and experiences that no one else is seeing. You drive streets, go to stores, walk neighborhoods, and have conversations with people that no one else on the planet is. You are the only one living the life you are living. No other person on the planet sees, hears, smells, tastes, and feels your life. Hence, no other person on the planet is experiencing what you are experiencing. In other words, you are seeing needs that no one else is seeing!

You live in a sea of uniqueness. This ecosystem of experience is filled with unique needs—needs that have to be filled and that no one else is noticing. Talk about noncompetition. What a tremendous opportunity! Actually, it is *your* opportunity. The universe is providing *you* with an opportunity that is strangely unique to you. Literally, no one else can fill the needs exactly as you can. You are powerful beyond belief.

Landvoice

It is appropriate at this point to tell you a little more about the business that allowed me to retire before I was forty. I relate this story to offer a true-life experience of the concepts discussed above. The lesson I learned is that you must pay attention. This story is nothing more than noticing a need and filling it. You can do exactly the same thing. Sure, there are many roads that may lead to success, but this is definitely one road that leads to the creation of a profitable and successful business. I know because I took it.

Real Estate Assistant

In the fall of 1990, I commenced graduate school at a local university. Having taken a job in retail management a few years earlier, I felt something was missing and quit that job to go to graduate school full time. But I desperately needed a way to support a young family while attending school. Real estate had always fascinated me, so I decided to get a real estate license. After passing state exams, I found a part-time job working for one of the most successful realtors in the state.

My real estate assistant job was relatively easy. Every morning, I was required to bring in every newspaper I could find in the city. This included the large daily papers, smaller weekly papers, community papers, and all free publications like the *Big Nickel*, the *Pennysaver*, and so on. I did so. My employer taught me how to go through the real estate section of each paper and identify which properties were being sold by owner. I was instructed to cut out these For Sale by Owner (FSBO) ads and place them in a unique 3x5 card file system that my employer called "The Goldmine." He had created a way to track every property that was For Sale by Owner in the area. Essentially, it was an FSBO multiple listing service.

The objective was straightforward. The moment any FSBO advertised in any public source anywhere, my boss wanted to know about it. The system was easy and amazing. As soon as I completed updating the FSBO list each morning, my employer and I, along with a few other assistants, would proceed to contact each of these home sellers. After asking a series of questions, we would make an appointment to tour each home. With this system alone, this particular realtor was listing three to five homes a day and somewhere between one hundred and one hundred fifty homes a month.

For those familiar with the real estate industry, you will recognize that these are spectacular numbers. This particular agent would sell, on average, eighty to one hundred homes a month. At the time, the average commission was about $3,000 per home. Therefore, he was generating income between $240,000 and $300,000 a month. Being somewhat eccentric, this particular agent enjoyed walking around the office with his daily commission checks totaling $10k to $15k dangling out of his shirt pocket.

I began asking questions.

- Do other realtors have a need for information like this?
- If so, how many other agents had systems in place to gather this sort of daily info?
- Did other real estate–oriented professionals (mortgage lenders, title agents, moving companies, and so on) have a need for this same type of information?

Having trained myself years earlier to pay attention to the needs of others, I quickly recognized that others might have a need that I could fill. It is interesting to consider why no one before I came along had considered setting up this particular type of business. This agent had hired many assistants before me. He had worked the system for years before my arrival. Many other real estate agents, brokers, assistants, and other real estate professionals were familiar with the success and systems of this particular agent. So why didn't any of these other individuals recognize the opportunity? I believe the answer is found in the very Success Tip we are now discussing. Simply, they had not trained themselves to consider the needs of others sufficiently. Immediately, I saw a need that was not readily apparent to others. A need I could fill.

This is why it is critical to train yourself to pay attention to the needs of others beginning immediately. Had all my interest and attention been all about my own success, I would have never realized the opportunity that was staring me in the face. There have been—and will continue to be—business opportunities right in front of you, but if you're not observant and aware, they will naturally remain untapped until one who is aware stumbles across the opportunity.

Shortly after recognizing the business opportunity that was in front of me, I quit this particular agent's employ. In leaving, I was honest and up front. I informed him of my intentions to start a business providing daily FSBO leads. Surprisingly, after he determined that it was more cost effective for him to buy the data from me rather than to hire personal assistants to gather this same info, he became one of my first clients. Ironically, I continued to fill his need while filling the needs of many others nationwide as well.

Unless you have been—or are presently—in a real estate profession, you most likely have not heard of the name Warnock's By Owner. We operated the business under the DBA Landvoice. Prior to recently selling the company, our company headquarters were in Salt Lake City, Utah. We employed between sixty and eighty employees at any one time and serviced over thirty thousand subscribers. The company typically enjoyed annual gross sales in excess of $6 million.

I started this business by doing nothing spectacular. I simply noticed and *filled a need*.

The Need Test

If you are serious about starting a business, begin by answering the below questions. This list of nine questions is what I call the Need Test. The objective of the questions is to focus your attention below the surface of your daily life so that you can more fully appreciate the dynamics that form the foundation of the particular needs at play in your world.

You will find it valuable to answer the below questions with one specific context in mind. For example, think of your favorite restaurant, your present or former workplace, or a hobby or pastime that you enjoy. Now answer the following questions, thinking specifically about that particular business, context, activity, or situation:

1. What products are produced? By whom? For whom?

2. What services are performed? By whom? For whom?
3. What operational systems are followed? By whom? For whom?
4. What information is obtained? By whom? For whom?
5. Who is preeminently performing services for this industry?
6. What makes them the best? What are they doing that others are not?
7. What is the need that is being filled? What benefits are clients receiving?
8. What needs are not being adequately filled? What is missing?
9. How can the service, product, system, information, or experience be improved?

You will note that the first two questions refer to products and services separately. In business conversations, these two terms often merge as if they are the same thing. They are not. Products and services are distinct and must be addressed separately. Most successful and unique businesses are built on filling a need differently based on a focus of either the service or the product. An example may help illustrate. Consider IKEA, the large Swiss-based retail furniture factory that has experienced tremendous growth in the last decade. They have similar products (assemble your own furniture) as many existing furniture stores. Success for IKEA was founded on developing an entirely different way of service (the customer is the warehouse worker).

As you answer the Need Test questions for your particular opportunity of interest, make sure you identify *both* the product—the "what," or the physical deliverable being provided—as well as the service—the "how," or the operational system at play that determines how the product is experienced.

You will notice that you can use the Need Test for any industry, situation, context, environment, or position you are experiencing in your world. Simply ask and answer the same nine questions for any particular context you like. If you use the above Need Test consistently, it is only a matter of time before you notice, identify, and realize a significant need that remains unfilled.

Just prior to starting Landvoice, I remember exactly where I was when the realization came to me that a unique opportunity was staring me in the face. For several weeks I had been asking and pondering about work using the above questions as a guide. One day, my wife picked me up from work. I jumped into the passenger seat and started talking to her about these issues when suddenly it hit me. It was as if a bright stream of light had come crashing right through the windshield. It illuminated my world and my mind. I experienced illuminated insight. This Need Test was the impetus for this amazing experience.

Most likely you have had a similar insight at one time or another. It is in these moments when almost miraculously you are able to connect the dots and align with a possibility that was nonexistent a few moments earlier. It is in these moments when unique and creative ideas are hatched. It is in these moments when genuine, unique, plausible possibilities come to mind. For me, the idea of beginning my particular business at that particular time was quite surreal. In that moment, for the first time, it occurred to me that the real estate information I gathered every day could be replicated, duplicated, and sold to agents worldwide. I experienced in that flash of light a life-changing moment. You can too!

I believe it may be worthwhile to repeat an earlier statement:

- I am not wise beyond my years.
- I am not more intelligent.
- I am not luckier.
- I am not from a wealthy background.
- It is actually not about me at all—nor is it about you.

"It" is about one simple action that you can begin doing today—*fill a need*!

SUCCESS TIP #1
FILL A NEED!

I present the remaining Success Tips in a chronological and progressive format. In other words, the Success Tips are presented in order of priority. As your business grows and becomes more established and successful, the latter Success Tips become more applicable. As outlined from the beginning, the purpose of this book is not a comprehensive A to Z guide on starting and running your own business. Rather, my intention is to share personal stories of business successes and failures, revealing critical Success Tips that make a difference between success and failure as you move forward, building your own successful business. At the very least, adherence to these critical Success Tips will save you considerable time and money.

SUCCESS TIP #2
HAVE YOU TASTED THE FRUITS OF PASSION?

"PASSION" IS ONE OF the most powerful words in the English language. In Christian theology, the word "passion" is attributed to the supernatural and central element of life. Synonyms with the word "passion" include words like "zeal," "fire," and "fervor." "Zeal" is a tireless devotion for a cause. "Fire" is a burning desire. "Fervor" refers to the intensity of feeling. In sum, passion is a feeling and emotion that masters the mind and moves the soul.

Consider a feeling that you have had previously that mastered (controlled) the mind. Most likely, it dealt with intense feelings of love (or passion) that you may have had for a loved one. Possibly, you felt passion in times of intense competition, during artistic or musical creation, while participating in an engaging interpersonal discussion, or while witnessing a memorable presentation. In each of these cases, passion is present when all other thoughts and feelings fade into the background and powerful, strong, compelling drive, desire, and devotion for a cause outside of yourself rule preeminent.

Let's be honest. We do not need to discuss passion at length. You are already familiar with it. You have had moments in your life when you felt this enormous shower of excitement for someone or something outside of yourself. This is passion. When the idea for Landvoice formed within me, I was so excited I could hardly keep still. The thoughts of this business became all-consuming. I was talking about it wildly with my wife, siblings, and anyone who would listen. The passion flowed through me. It was not something that needed measuring. It did not need studying or articulation. It just was. Passion is accompanied by euphoria, an undeniable excitement for what may be.

The Passion Test

In your pursuit to fill the needs of others, you begin to notice, reflect on, and entertain many worthwhile business ideas and possibilities. Though many of these ideas are worthy of pursuit, it is imperative that you invest your limited time and finite energy to those ideas that you are most passionate about. I suggest that before engaging in any new business venture, you ask yourself some questions to help clarify if the particular opportunity you are pondering is worthy of pursuit.

I refer to these questions as the Passion Test. While thinking specifically about a particular potential business endeavor, answer the following questions:

1. Do you feel excited about the potential?
2. Do you feel that others—clients, employees, and partners—can become excited about the idea as well?
3. Do you feel that you could comfortably involve yourself in this business for years to come?
4. Do you feel that every aspect of this idea is aligned with who you are and what you hope to accomplish in the future?
5. Do you feel more excited about this opportunity than any other opportunity you are presently aware of?
6. Do you feel you could commit your full-time energies to this opportunity should it be required?

The purpose of taking the Passion Test is to determine whether *you feel* a particular endeavor is worth doing. It is not by accident that each of the questions of the Passion Test begins with the statement "Do you feel." Passion is intensely personal. Passion is something you feel. You cannot talk yourself into passion. You cannot earn passion. You cannot purchase passion. You cannot learn passion. You cannot create passion. You cannot steal passion.

Passion is something you either have or do not have for a particular person or cause. Passion springs from your inner core. It is a sign of energy that is deep within you. Passion is comparable to oil buried deep in an aquifer under the surface of the earth. The evidence of passion is evidence of personal energy that can deliver huge returns. I am constantly reminding my children to feel and to trust their feelings more than their thoughts. "Trust your feelings," I consistently exhort them, "for your body knows more than your mind can possibly comprehend." Our minds are constantly racing, creating, worrying, fearing, debating, and justifying. Our minds are in constant, nonstop commotion. In many respects, our minds are a disease. They create worlds that are not so. They create problems that are nonexistent. They create fears to defend egos. So, trust your body. Feel! Our bodies feel far beyond the limitations of our minds. When in doubt, when confused, when unsure, follow your feelings.

It is important to note that the mere presence of passion does not necessarily mean that a particular business will deliver huge returns. However, and more importantly, the evidence of passion proves that you do possess an essential ingredient needed for success. As the great German philosopher George Wilhelm Friedrich Hegel once said, "Nothing great in the world has ever been accomplished without passion."[1] Passion (energy) is required for accomplishment. If you have passion, this trait alone can carry you a long, long way toward your goals.

Passion for Landvoice

Two quick examples may help illuminate. When I began Landvoice nearly twenty years ago, I could answer unequivocally "yes" to every one of the above Passion Test questions. If you are pondering engaging in a particular business endeavor or major life decision and you can unequivocally answer "yes" to all of the questions of the Passion Test, you are headed in the right direction.

Passion for Sweet & Sassy

Unlike Landvoice, however, I recently engaged in another business endeavor that ended much differently. The primary reason, I believe, was a lack of passion. This particular business endeavor also had the potential to be enormously successful. I took the Passion Test for this particular business and was able to answer questions 1 through 5 in the affirmative. However, I was unable to answer question number 6 of the Passion Test affirmatively. Question number 6 asks: "Do you feel you could commit your full time energies to this opportunity should it be required?"

My wife and I began this new business with the desire to be absentee owners. Given our financial situation, proximity to the store, and many other business interests, neither my wife nor I had any real interest or desire in committing full time to this new opportunity. It was simply a fun enterprise.

Unfortunately, I chose to ignore this particular question in the Passion Test, and we began the new business anyway. I rationalized that I could manage this new enterprise from a distance and that I would never need to dedicate my full-time energies. What I failed to realize at the time was that my inability to answer "yes" for all the questions in the Passion Test revealed a lack of passion for this particular business.

My unwillingness to acknowledge that I may be required to commit enormous energy to the enterprise reflected a lack of passion, energy, and commitment. I wish I had paid attention to this red flag before engaging in this new endeavor. Six months into operations, it was clear that the business model required more time commitments and financial investment than I was prepared to assume.

With the support of my wife, we decided to sell the store for a loss. We were physically, emotionally, and financially unwilling to commit our full-time energies to this endeavor. Ironically, both my wife and I know that had either of us been willing to invest full-time energies—even if just for a short time—we could have created the systems necessary for success. Both of us were unwilling and unmotivated to do so.

In business, a lack of passion can lead to tremendous financial losses. It did for us. Such an emotional and financial loss can easily be prevented by responding honestly to the Passion Test before starting an enterprise.

SUCCESS TIP #2
ENGAGE WITH PASSION!

Note

1. George Wilhelm Friedrich Hegel, *Lectures on the Philosophy of History*, trans. J. Sibree (New York: Dover, 1956).

SUCCESS TIP #3
IS SIMPLE SWEET?

Company A or Company B?

Consider the following scenario:

In the first month of operations, Company A acquires six clients, brings in monthly revenues of only $240, but has no debt and no expenses.

In comparison, Company B in the first month of operations obtains one hundred clients, has monthly revenues approaching $30,000, and has debt in excess of $600,000, with monthly expenses in excess of $50,000.

Which business would you prefer?

It is tempting to argue that Company B, with the larger numbers of clients and more revenue is the preferred company.

The above scenario is not fictional. These are the actual first month financial numbers from two different businesses that I began. Which of these two businesses do you suppose provides the income that allowed my early retirement, Company A or Company B? In addition, in which company did I lose $200,000 in the first year of operation and ultimately sell for a loss? The answer is obvious isn't it? It is impossible to lose $200,000 in operations and sell a company for a loss if you have no debt and little expenses. Yes, it is Company A, Landvoice, that allowed me to retire early. It was Company B, a Sweet & Sassy franchise, in which I invested huge sums of money in a concept I believed had huge potential but ultimately lost hundreds of thousands of dollars.

The inherent value in starting simple and inexpensive is powerful. If every dollar earned is truly a dollar earned, not a dollar going to pay off accrued debt, you are the winner. For a new business, this win is huge. It does not matter what the win is. I hope you realize the importance of this statement. It does not matter if the win is a large, multimillion-dollar contract or a small, ten-dollar sale. The important point is that the win only occurs when you collect more than you expend.

Through personal experience I have learned, as have thousands of other entrepreneurs, that beginning a business with hundreds of thousands of dollars of debt takes all the fun, passion, energy, and love out of the equation. Regardless of whether you have money to invest or not and regardless of whether it is your first business adventure or your fifty-second, I would strongly encourage you to begin all of your business ventures simple and inexpensive. If you truly want to be successful in your next business endeavor, pretend like you have nothing but your time. If every dollar of revenue collected is a dollar earned, how joyous is the return. It is the feeling of winning that will drive the business to the next level. Success breeds success.

Please understand that I am not suggesting that an investment of capital into a new venture is a business killer. There definitely will be an appropriate time to invest heavily in the expansion of your business. There will be an appropriate time to consider receiving a cash infusion from savings, investors, or loans. I am simply suggesting that such investments are made only *after* needs are identified and products or services have been proven to effectively and profitably fill a need.

If you can run your business profitably with no debt and little expenses—regardless of how small or little that profit may be—you get a glimpse of its potential. When you start with nothing, everything is a profit. Everything is a win. When you experience a win, your passion and excitement are renewed.

In terms of the Company B scenario mentioned above (Sweet & Sassy), it is important to ask what happened. Why did the original passion, excitement, and energy dissipate? The answer is simple: a lack of wins. Though we continually received franchiser recognition for outstanding sales and revenues, the revenues simply did not keep up with expenses. We spent more money (lots more) each month than we collected.

It did not matter what we did to cut costs. Nothing helped. We laid off employees. We cut advertising. We scaled back retail orders. Eventually, the realization began to set in that we had invested too much in the initial start-up and revenues could not keep up with both operational and debt expenses. While immersed in this financial travesty, I truly discovered how quickly financial losses can dissipate passion, energy, and enjoyment for a business. You who have been there know exactly what I mean.

We live in an age when bigger seems better. Too many entrepreneurs now think they need to come in big, with a bang, investing huge sums of money in technology, software, office space, personnel, retail locations, warehouses, and marketing strategies—all before they even know if they have a viable service and product. I implore you, however, to keep it simple. Start inexpensive. You will learn soon enough if there is a need and a demand requiring larger investments. The importance and ramifications of this Success Tip cannot be overstated.

When we began Landvoice, we started this business in our kitchen. I honestly believe this is a significant reason that we were ultimately successful. We used our home phone as the business line. We refused to purchase a fax machine necessary for distributing our daily lead information until we had six signed and committed paying customers. It worked wonders. Within a few days I had officially signed up the first six subscribers to the service. We then purchased a fax machine and formally began delivering the service. With no overhead, a business can thrive. You are probably familiar with the many stories of highly successful companies that started literally out of a garage or apartment.

Google was founded in a dorm room and later in a garage.

Dell computer was founded with $1,000 in start-up capital.

Microsoft began with no overhead, making their first deal in a hotel room in Albuquerque, New Mexico.

YouTube began in a garage in Menlo Park, California, when three friends were talking about a party they had gone to the night before, had videotaped some of the party, and needed a way to share it with their friends.

Ben and Jerry opened up their first ice cream store in an old, abandoned gas station in Vermont.

It is not by accident that many of the world's largest and most successful companies first began their operations small, simple, and inexpensive. Beginning a business with no overhead, no employees, no commitments, no legal contracts, no partners, and no outside investors allows you the ultimate freedom. You have no one to answer to, no one to report to, and no one to change your mind or unnecessarily influence your decisions.

Starting small and inexpensive is the safest way to start any enterprise. When you start a business inexpensively, consider what your ultimate risk is. It is your time. Is it possible that you end up investing a lot of time into this new enterprise only to see it fail? Absolutely! Is it likewise possible that you end up investing a lot of time into this enterprise only to see it soar to success? Of course! The unknowns drive the entrepreneur. The possibilities are the fruits of the labor. Consider the following formula for success:

NEED + PASSION + TIME = SUCCESS

Your time combined with your passion focused on a need that you can fill is the formula for business success. Do you honestly believe that it is simply luck that enabled simple and inexpensive start-ups to grow to mega proportions? Early wins mean everything!

SUCCESS TIP #3
START SIMPLE AND INEXPENSIVE!

SUCCESS TIP #4
HARD WORK—REALLY?

Sweet & Sassy

In 2005, life was great. The economy was strong, my businesses were creating a profit fit for a king, and I was retired. Having a bit too much free time, I began looking at other businesses to start. It was at this time that I purchased the before-mentioned Sweet & Sassy franchise. Sweet & Sassy is a salon, retail outlet, and party place for girls ages two through twelve. The concept was fantastic. I fell in love with the idea, especially since there were no similar places presently in the area. I determined, using the Needs Test, that this business definitely filled a need. As previously mentioned, I opened the store with the intention of being an absentee owner. I loved the idea but had no interest in working in the store myself. The failed venture proved extremely costly in both money and time.

I have since wondered why I was so unwilling to do the hard work myself. I believe it was pride. I felt I was too important and my time was too valuable to work in the establishment myself. My time was too valuable. Why would I work the front counter when I could hire someone for $8 an hour to do it? I had no interest in working personally with the employees, handling customer complaints, or stocking shelves. I had many other more important things going on in my world. Working retail was definitely not part of the equation. In hindsight, how I wish I had humbled myself, taken my own advice, and done the hard work myself initially.

Before starting Sweet & Sassy, I had never owned a retail operation and was unaccustomed to many of the nuances of the industry. When issues, questions, and decisions had to be made, I was entirely dependent on the opinion and experience of the store manager. I quickly discovered that attempting to successfully run an enterprise without personal experience in the day-to-day operations of the business is like flying a plane without any training. You may believe you have an effectively trained copilot, but if you are not personally familiar with the controls, the dashboard, and the functions of the aircraft, you are in for a turbulent, if not potentially disastrous, flight.

My wife and I have spent countless hours discussing the age-old question "what might have been." What could we have created had we been willing to humble ourselves and run this store—at least for a short time? The irony is humorous. Had I been willing to do the initial hard work myself, I would have actually spent far fewer hours on the venture than I did anyway. Moreover, the hours that I would have invested would have been focused on the creation of effective systems rather than cleaning up a disastrous accident. As it was, I lost a tremendous amount of time, energy, and money on a failed enterprise. I hope that after reading this book, you will choose to avoid making similar costly mistakes.

Assigning someone else to do the hard work initially will prove painful and unsuccessful. In the end, you will most likely find that you are either forced to take over the hard work yourself anyway or forced out of business entirely. From personal experience, I would suggest the first path is best. Avoid the pain and misery and prepare to do the hard work yourself.

Mentos

I really like those chewy mint candies called Mentos. The love affair began years ago when I was about nine years old. At church, one of my Sunday School teachers introduced these new candies to our class. She would reward us with Mentos for right answers, quiet behavior, and so on. Even to this day, I carry Mentos with me wherever I go. I have a stash in my office, home, and car. Similar to my teacher long ago, I constantly offer Mentos to my classes at school and church, to my neighbors, and to my children's friends. Our home is known as the Mentos haven at Halloween. For this reason, I am often called "Mentos Man" by children who know me best.

A few years ago, I was visiting my son's class, and they invited me to participate in a teachers versus students game of kick ball. Whenever it was my turn to kick, some of the neighbor kids would scream out, "Go Mentos Man!" After the game, the principal came up and asked in all sincerity, "Do you own the Mentos company?"

Jordan's Mentos Route

This interest in Mentos created a business opportunity for my oldest son. One day I was surfing the web for new business ideas, and a pop-up ad with a bright blue Mentos vending machine caught my eye. I was intrigued. *This may be a perfect first business adventure for my son*, I thought. At the time, he was about thirteen. I showed him the concept; we discussed it and ordered twenty machines.

I knew at the beginning of this adventure that it would require some time. Little did I realize what I was actually getting myself into. Neither of us took the passion test at the time. We should have! When the time comes around each month to service the machines, my son and I both groan a bit.

The plan was to hire a locator company who, for a fee, would place the machines at different locations. We have been through no less than three different placement agencies thus far. We have not found one who fulfilled their promise. It was a nightmare. It's been four years since we purchased the machines, and we have only half the machines placed. We still have eight new, never opened machines taking up space in our storage room. I have so many other things on my plate that I simply have no time or desire to make any placement calls myself. For this particular business, I have little interest in doing the hard work myself.

Besides the aforementioned difficulties, however, the opportunity to spend four or five hours with my son in the car each month is priceless. We actually have a great time when we get out servicing the machines, counting the money, filling out reports, and talking business. I also enjoy seeing the satisfaction on my son's face when the restaurant owners and customers ask him questions about his business. It also makes me smile when he finishes his reports. Every month he reports to me, with a big grin on his face, that he made about $30 per hour for his efforts. Indeed, business ownership has its benefits.

Landvoice

Earlier I shared the story of how I launched Landvoice, the real estate lead generation service. It needs to be stated clearly that there is one main reason that Landvoice turned into a multi-million dollar venture: hard work. For the first few years, my wife and I woke up at 5:00 every morning to ensure that our clients received the best possible information in a timely manner and without interruption. Oftentimes, during those first few years, we worked straight through the night. Initially, we sacrificed weekends, vacations, family parties, and other holidays to guarantee quality control. As the only sales person initially, I made forty to fifty phone calls a day to real estate professionals informing them about our service. Did I enjoy this? Not always. But I was following the prescribed system for success. I had identified a need that I could fill. I was passionate about the service. I started small and inexpensive, and I was willing to do the hard work myself. Adhering to the first four principles discussed in this book has made all the difference.

Many people want to start and own their own business for a variety of reasons; flexibility, freedom, control, power, wealth, and so on. Nevertheless, I am convinced that many believe owning your own business means you can do less work. This may be true in the long run, but do not be mistaken. It will require considerable work, at least initially, to get to that point.

You may be reading this book because you are a business owner, a manager, or a president of a large corporation. Possibly you work for someone else but find yourself in a leadership role as a departmental manager, a supervisor, or a team lead, or you may simply have a desire to run your own business in the near future. If any of these apply to you, you are already a leader. You desire to be the commander rather than a foot soldier. You prefer being a chief rather than an Indian. Owning your own business indeed has benefits. Eventually, when your business is humming like a fine-tuned Ferrari, you will enjoy all the benefits of business ownership.

It is imperative that you launch a business with your eyes wide open. If you intend to enjoy all the benefits of business ownership, you must be willing to pay the price—initially. In other words, you must be willing to do the hard work yourself at the beginning.

What is the hard work? For this present discussion, the hard work can be defined as all business-related tasks essential for the successful operation of the business. It often involves the uncomfortable possibility of rejection, intense communication, difficult conversations, and possibly misunderstandings.

It may prove helpful to clearly delineate the seven elements of the above definition of hard work. Hard work

- Includes all tasks
- Is essential for operations
- Requires intense time
- Requires intense energy
- Involves possible rejection
- Includes possible intense communication
- Involves possible misunderstanding

Given the above seven features of what it means to be

willing to do the hard work yourself, it is safe to assume that there is no job that you, as the owner, should not be prepared to tackle, at least initially. Regardless of the time, energy, or expertise involved, it is imperative that you be willing to jump in with both feet and get wet. Once you have learned and recorded the nuances of each particular task, you can then move on. It is important to emphasize that there are essentially two very different yet interconnected types of hard work: creation and implementation.

The first type of hard work involves the creation of effective systems. The Success Tip that we are presently discussing—do the hard work initially—is all about the first type of hard work: creation. When you are willing to jump in and learn the basic functions of each task, you then learn what is necessary to create the operational steps for success. The second type of hard work, the implementation of systems, is discussed in the next chapter.

The Creation of Effective Systems

It is critical as you start a new business that you be willing, at least for a time, to get hands-on experience in every aspect of the business you embark upon. Doing the hard work yourself, at least initially, means that you must plan on being intensely involved in every aspect of your business from the outset. Do not be afraid to jump in with both feet. Do not hesitate. This is your business. Make it yours by investing your time and energy in the most important aspects of the company procedures. Since this is your business, it is imperative that you learn every aspect of it. Become fully immersed in all tasks essential for the successful operation of the enterprise. It is invaluable for you to spend a few days answering phones, interacting with customers, handling complaints, washing, cooking, cleaning, serving, selling, and participating in all other operations to thoroughly educate yourself with all elements of the enterprise.

You may be asking, "Why is it so important that I do the

hard work myself? Why would I spend time answering phones, working the front counter, handling customer complaints, signing up subscribers, selling and marketing, and so forth? My time is much too valuable for that. I can hire employees far cheaper who can do that work more effectively than I can." Have you seen the relatively new reality TV show entitled *Undercover Boss*? It is a show that depicts senior management executives from some of the nation's largest corporations who spend a day working incognito in some of the blue collar jobs inside their companies. It is fascinating to see the realization and understanding that naturally flow when a manager, CEO, president, or owner realizes the work, the systems, the inefficiencies of the day-to-day operations of an enterprise. Imagine the value of being familiar with the majority of the business operations firsthand and of being involved in the creation of systems of success.

Remember, when you are doing the hard work, you are doing more than just the hard work. Literally, you are creating the systems and procedures that all future employees will use to do these tasks in the most efficient and effective way possible. Doing the hard work yourself ensures that you truly understand the best practices and systems required for your business to succeed.

The initial time that you invest in doing what you may deem as hourly wage responsibilities will save you more than you may now appreciate. The time you spend with your "hands on the wheel" of each position enables you to adequately learn the business from all perspectives. We learn by making mistakes, by saying the wrong things, by losing sales, by falling down. We learn when we get discouraged and disappointed and by getting dog tired. The few hours or days you invest hands-on in every aspect of your enterprise will teach you the nuances of success. T.D. Jakes, a successful author and motivational speaker, often emphasizes in his books and presentations that "our greatest lessons in life are most often learned by mistakes."[1]

Indeed, if you commit to doing the hard work yourself, one day you will look back fondly at those days and say, "those days that I spent doing the hard work were probably the most important days I spent starting this company." I unequivocally affirm that doing the hard work yourself may well be the difference between ultimate long-term success and failure.

Initially.

Notice that I have indicated throughout this section that to be truly successful, you must do the hard work yourself—initially. "Initially" is the key word. There will come a time when you will be ready to pass the hard work off to others. Once you have created the operational systems, fine-tuned the operational processes, and distributed the critical knowledge important for the smooth operation of your business, it's time to pass those responsibilities on to others. The next Success Tip, "Ensure Systems Are Created, Recorded, and Followed," will discuss this next stage in depth. It is at this point that you really begin to enjoy the benefits of business ownership.

SUCCESS TIP #4
DO THE HARD WORK YOURSELF–INITIALLY!

Note

1. T.D. Jakes, *Reposition Yourself: Living Life without Limits* (New York: Simon & Schuster, 2007).

SUCCESS TIP #5
SO WHAT ABOUT SYSTEMS?

Three Bags

While in graduate school, I read about a professor who came to class one day carrying three large paper bags in his arms. After setting them on his desk, he began by asking the students a simple question: "What is similar about these three entities?" He then reached into one of the bags and carefully lifted out a live crab. He placed it on his desk. Next, he reached into a second bag and brought out a large globe of the earth. From the third sack, he pulled out a large portrait of his family. Again, he asked, "What is similar about these three entities?"

The class was quiet for a time. Then hesitantly a few answers began to trickle in. "They all are colorful" volunteered one student. "They all are living objects," guessed another. Not getting the answer he was looking for, the professor eventually answered his own question. "Each of these three entities is a system. Everything we see, experience, know, and understand is a system. A system is a collection of interdependent parts that function together to create a unique whole."

Business Is a System

There are many subtle yet powerful insights that an intense study of systems would illuminate for a business owner. Such a study could be a natural sequel to this book. For the present discussion, the creation of a profitable business is nothing more than the creation and repetition of successful, proven systems that fill a need. Michael Gerber, author of the E-myth, has outlined these procedures in detail. I highly recommend you read his book *The E-myth Revisited: Why Most Small Businesses Don't Work and What to Do about It.*

If you follow the four Success Tips I have outlined in this book thus far—"Fill a Need," "Engage with Passion," "Start Simple and Inexpensive," and "Do the Hard Work Yourself—Initially"—you will already have systems in place that need recording. In terms of business operations, a system is an instructional guide explaining in detail how each aspect of your business is to be handled.

Operational Journal

If you have been in business for more than a month and have generated revenue of any sort, you now have instructions that need to be recorded. Recording your ongoing daily business practices is what I will refer to as an operational journal. The operational journal covers all aspects of your business, including sales and marketing, accounting, invoicing, bill paying, customer service, handling objections, phone etiquette, technology, and vendor relations. In essence, it details every task involved in the operation of your business.

It is common for small business owners to not fully appreciate how valuable their insight and detailed instructions are to the eventual success of their company. You may view the steps that you have done in building your business as common sense, simple, and obvious. However, beware of the humility fallacy. Do not discount what you have learned through doing the hard work yourself. Trial and error is the greatest of teachers. If you have sales revenue, regardless of how small or large the dollar volumes, you are running a business. It is critical that you record all your activities in an operational journal.

This operational journal should be a free-flowing document

in which you record five elements of your ongoing business practices:

- What you did
- When you did it
- What the results were
- What you learned
- What you suggest for the future

Recording your business experiences is vital to ensure that lessons learned are not forgotten in the future. This operational journal is the foundation for your future operational manuals. It will provide a wealth of information that can be referred to continually by management. In essence, the operational journal is the Book of Business Life. It should be kept in a three-ring binder and displayed for all to access.

Just as you would do in a personal journal, I suggest you record the date and time of every entry. Also, provide headings to indicate the specific topic you are writing about. In sum, this journal should be a brief recording of what you are doing and learning in each aspect of your business. Also, record what you are undertaking that is new and the subsequent results of your tests. It is a powerful record of what worked, what did not work, and what you have discovered about your particular business and industry.

Landvoice's Lack of an Operational Journal

I personally managed and operated Landvoice for thirteen years, 1990 to 2003. In that time, we doubled both gross and net revenues every year. In 2003, I became tired and burned out. I decided to step down and stop managing the day-to-day affairs of the company. I hired a new company president to replace me who appeared very promising. He possessed energy, excitement, and passion.

In hindsight, I now recognize that I had passed him the torch without one essential ingredient necessary for success:

direction. Though I managed the business for thirteen years and possessed a good working knowledge on every aspect of the business, I had not diligently recorded my experiences in an operational journal. I assumed that anyone with common sense could take over and do what I did. I learned the hard way that business success is not simply about common sense.

For eighteen months, I watched as this promising young talent ran my company nearly into the ground. Overall, gross revenues dropped 20 percent over an eighteen-month span. Net revenues decreased by a whopping 40 percent. Total company expenditures increased 20 percent. Employee morale and turnover increased at an alarming rate. The company lost nearly every loyal employee that had worked for me over the past thirteen years. New employees who had no interest, appreciation, or knowledge of the historical lessons learned replaced the once loyal, knowledgeable, and dedicated staff.

Because of the lack of a detailed operational journal, each department from sales, accounting, customer support, and technology were left to their own imaginations and interests. It should not surprise you to learn that the company that once collected over $6 million in annual revenues and earned over $1 million in net revenues nearly collapsed in less than eighteen months.

In hindsight, it is clear I made two crucial mistakes in the process of becoming an absentee owner. The first mistake, as I mentioned, was that I did not make a detailed operational journal available for referencing. The second mistake was not giving strict instructions that all new managers should follow the valuable lessons learned in thirteen years of operation. Lessons previously learned are effective signposts paving the way for future decision-makers toward the path of prosperity and away from the path of pain and loss.

It is important to realize that an operational journal is a living document. By this, I mean that the operational journal is never a completed document. It is continually open to new entries. It should be understood by management that the policies presently adhered to will continue until it can be proven, over time, that there are new procedures and systems more effective than the past systems.

New ideas will appear and new technologies will be introduced. New and more efficient marketing methods and systems will be created and new solutions will be conceived. New cost-reducing technologies will surface. It is important to be open to new suggestions. Yet it is just as important to ensure that lessons learned in the past are continually shared and respected in the present and future. You have invested a lot of time and money into lessons learned and effective systems created. Do not allow effective systems to be thrown into the trash until new and improved systems and suggestions are proven effective.

Unbelievably, in the past I allowed my sales and marketing departments to terminate successful, revenue-building marketing strategies for a promise of even better results from new and promising, but unproven, technologically oriented sales systems. Not once have these promising new techniques compensated for the loss of growth we encountered by discontinuing the systems that were effective.

Similarly, I have allowed my accounting and technology departments to implement grandiose proposals and drop existing practices only to later regret my decisions. It is not that new methods are always unsuccessful. It's just a fact that unproven new methods are rarely immediately successful. Fundamentally, new systems and techniques take more time, more investment, and more capital than originally planned. Do not drop the old for the new without sufficient proof, over time, that the new approaches, systems, technologies, or advances will outperform the old systems. In addition, it's always wise to ensure that the proven systems are continued while simultaneously implementing the new.

New School versus Old School

Landvoice was founded and built on a simple two-pillared marketing strategy. For simplicity, these two strategies are referred to as internal and external sales. On one hand, we grew the business internally and independently. We did this by utilizing an inside sales team. Each team member was required to consistently contact fifty new potential clients a day. Each team member understood the necessity of new contacts. Regardless of what else was happening in the office, these outbound sales calls were completed each day. It did not matter how busy they were, how many incoming calls were handled, or what other crises or excuses came up, each was accountable for keeping the incoming pipeline flowing by making the fifty required calls per day.

The second sales strategy employed was externally focused. The external strategy involved collaborating with other companies within the industry. We called these external companies "gatekeepers" and often referred to them as affiliates. Success Tip #8 speaks in detail about the importance of gatekeeper partnerships. It is important to note that these two sales strategies enabled Landvoice to double in size *every year* for ten straight years.

With growth comes the need for new people, and eventually we hired an experienced and previously successful marketing manager. This new manager, however, was trained differently. He mocked our old school approach and introduced new visions based on technology, information, and internet usage. He was persuasive. Soon we turned all our attention and resources to these technologies. A few hundred thousand dollars later, it was clear that the return on investment (ROI) for these new strategies was far inferior to our original model. We had expended huge resources for minimal returns. We lost literally thousands of potential subscribers and hundreds of thousands of dollars in revenue during this ill-fated change of focus.

We live in a world of technology. It is relatively easy to hide behind technology. We all want to believe that technology will solve all our problems without realizing the limits and side effects of such advances. It is similar to the hope that modern medicine will destroy all future sickness and disease. There are unforeseen costs, side effects, and problems with new medical technologies just as there are with all new business-related technologies.

My Daughter Texting

The other day my daughter was texting her best friend. She had communicated something about going out with a particular boy, and her friend had become jealous and upset. After twenty minutes of escalated text messages, my daughter walked into my office in tears. In great despair, she told me that she was afraid she had permanently ruined her relationship with her best friend.

I asked her if she had thought of calling and talking personally to this friend. She stared at me with a bewildered look on her face. It was obvious she had not thought of this. She left, considering the suggestion. A few minutes later, she reappeared at the door of my office and informed me that she had called her friend, they had a great talk, all was fine, and she was going over to her friend's house to visit.

As she left, I thought of how many times we do just that in business. We email sales proposals. We set up social networking solutions. We set up links on our home pages. We create virtual brochures. We hide our clients inside contact management systems. We diligently assign account numbers to every client. Yet how often do we take the time to bypass automation and personally and sincerely communicate with our clients, partners, vendors, and affiliates?

In an article appropriately entitled "So Many Messages and So Little Time," Ginsberg reported on a research study that observed over one thousand employees from Fortune 1,000 companies. The intent of the study was to discover how much time the average US worker spends on incoming emails and voicemails. The results were astounding. Researchers discovered that the average employee receives over 178 messages daily, mostly email messages.[1] If it took just two minutes to deal with each message, the average American employee spends nearly six hours a day responding to emails and voicemails. In other words, on average, we spend 75 percent of our work time involved in technological transmissions. Technology is a great bridge, but be careful, for oftentimes technology is a great divide. If not monitored carefully, technology can have vast negative and unintended consequences.

The task of training each departmental manager to reference, utilize, and update the operational journal is yours—at least initially. This particular task should not be assigned to anyone else. As you start your business, you may not have any employees. Yet as your business grows, you will need to ensure that your personnel are trained properly on how to reference and use the operational journal. In fact, this may be the only training you need to provide. If your managers and employees understand your expectations as specified in the operational journal, you will find yourself enjoying the peaceful benefits of your operational journal entries.

It may surprise you how smooth your business will run when an operating system of proven policies and procedures are abided by. An observable system allows you to avoid many of the recurring exploratory expenses associated with most businesses. When approached with a new, creative, exciting, technologically advanced procedure or tool, you can simply refer the employee to the company's operational journal to see what has been learned previously. Often they will find past trials of similar programs recorded and will either abandon the proposal altogether or will offer a revised proposal based on what has been learned in the past.

Fortunately, I learn from my mistakes. After discovering

the problems at Landvoice, I immediately cleaned house. I hired new managers who readily agreed to follow the successful operations in place years earlier. I stepped back into the operations for a time to ensure that established, proven systems were strictly adhered to. One year later, we were enjoying the financial benefits of a profitable and successful company, humming like a fine-tuned Ferrari.

SUCCESS TIP #5
ENSURE SYSTEMS ARE CREATED, RECORDED, AND FOLLOWED!

Note

1. Steven Ginsberg, "So Many Messages and So Little Time," *Business Outlook*, May 5, 1997, C1.

SUCCESS TIP #6
WHY QUESTIONS?

A FEW YEARS AGO, I purchased a six-acre estate lot on the hills over-looking my hometown. At the time, it was one of the most expensive pieces of land in the city. They were asking nearly half a million for the property. I was prepared to pay that amount if required, though I was hoping to negotiate the price down, at least a little. When my wife and I sat down in the real estate agent's office and began talking price, rather than immediately offering my thoughts on what we were willing to pay, I simply asked a question:

"What do you feel is the lowest price the seller will take?"

His answer surprised me. "$425,000," he said.

We purchased the property for $425,000 and saved nearly $75,000 by doing nothing more than asking a question rather than openly revealing our initial thoughts and opinions. Asking questions allows others to reveal their thoughts, atti-tudes, hopes, desires, and, of course, needs. Humans naturally crave opportunities to speak and to be heard. Asking questions allows you to understand the situation before speaking. It is a critical step in becoming aware of another's attitude, position, expectations, hopes, desires, and needs.

Content and Relational Communication

Nearly every day as my children leave for school, I hug them and remind them to ask lots of questions. Communication is the most powerful tool we humans possess. We literally are

61

creators. We create everything around us, including our relationships with others, by how we choose to communicate with them. And asking questions is the most powerful communication tool we possess. Asking questions moves us beyond our own wisdom, thoughts, and feelings and merges those with the wisdom, thoughts, and feelings of others.

Asking questions is a co-creative process. By asking questions, we literally change our world. We invite a merger to occur between our thoughts and feelings and those of others. Asking questions encourages others to open up. It encourages others to participate, to be involved, and to be heard. Most importantly, asking questions reveals that we truly value the other and their opinion.

Early in my studies at the University of Utah, I was introduced to the concept that communication occurs on at least two levels: content and relational. In every communication instance, you reveal information to those with whom you are relating on both content and relational levels. Content level communication is the topic you are discussing; in other words, the information being exchanged. It is, however, the relational level of communication that is much more subtle and vastly more important. It is the more powerful and influential aspect of communication. In every word we say and every behavior we do, we reveal to others, "this is how I see you in relation to me." We reveal volumes to each other about how we see each other while we talk about the weather, business, school, work, food, and millions of other everyday topics.

Our First Fight

Nearly twenty years ago, I married my wife, Kathie. After the wedding ceremony, we enjoyed a two-week honeymoon and then returned home to our jobs and school. One particular morning, about a week after we had returned from the honeymoon, my wife mentioned that she had noticed that the red oil light in the car came on, indicating it was time for an oil change. She said she would do that on the way home from work. "Great," I said as I kissed her and left for work, not thinking much about it.

The day dragged on, and I was excited when it was time to return home. It is interesting how long those first few days apart seem after being married. When I arrived home, I excitedly ran up the stairs and hugged her. There we were, kissing, hugging, making out as only newlyweds could, when, in between kisses, she said:

"Oh, by the way, I changed the oil in the car today."

"Thanks," I said. "Did everything go OK?"

"Yes—no problem," she responded, "except the mechanic did suggest that we change the air filter."

Upon hearing this, I suddenly stepped back, and my entire demeanor changed as I asked rather judgmentally and in a firm voice, "*What?*"

Feeling the change in my demeanor, she hesitantly responded, "Well, he took the air filter out and showed me that it was pretty dirty. It was only $16."

Without thinking, I responded angrily, "*Only $16?*"

I was getting angrier by the moment. "Dang it, Kathie! What the . . . Ahh! Don't you know that every time you go get your oil changed they tell you that you need a new air filter? It's an up-sell. You can just blow the thing clean with an air hose. You don't need to buy a new one!"

To emphasize my anger, I swatted and punched wildly in the air.

This was the first time I raised my voice and revealed signs of anger toward my wife. How do you suppose she responded? Yep! She stood there and looked at me, bewildered, with large, frightened eyes, and then burst into uncontrollable tears, ran into the bedroom, and slammed and locked the door.

As with every communication event we engage in, this exchange altered our relationship forever. No, we did not divorce. Eventually she opened the door and we talked.

However, she had seen and felt something I could never take back. She had seen how I relationally valued her.

On a relational level, I revealed to my wife that I valued $16 more than I valued her. I also subtly communicated to her that I saw her as uninformed and naïve. This was revealed by my using phrases like "don't you know" where I clearly put her down, suggesting that I had knowledge that she did not have but I expected her to have.

How different the above situation could have been had I asked her questions before spitting out my own thoughts and opinions. By asking questions, we show that we value the other person, what they are thinking, and how they are seeing the world. Had I begun this exchange by asking sincere questions in an honest attempt to understand rather than to be understood, the entire communicative situation would have been vastly different.

Metaphor of Driving

Asking questions in conversations is similar to paying attention to other drivers while driving on a freeway. Safe and effective drivers crave information. Safe drivers understand how important it is to know what is going on all around them. They read signs. They look in blind spots. They check their mirrors. They look far down the road for possible hazards. Decisions are made based on observations. Though these types of drivers have an idea what is the best possible route to get to a particular destination, they remain flexible. They understand that other cars on the road, construction, accidents, emergencies, detours, and traffic congestion may affect the decisions they make while en route.

An effective driver does not simply decide to change lanes without paying attention to the road, other vehicles, their speed and proximity, space, traffic lights, brake lights, and so on. They appropriately make choices in the moment based on the information they receive by being aware of their environment.

It seems as though there are fewer safe and effective drivers on the road these days, and there seems to be just as few educated communicators.

Human Highways

Most of us simply do not pay sufficient attention to others around us as we navigate human highways. We often choose to "change lanes," making comments, sharing opinions, and revealing our own thoughts, before gathering all the necessary information from those around us so we can make better and more informed decisions. Effective communicators, like effective drivers, make decisions only after researching the surroundings thoroughly. Asking questions is the most powerful tool we humans possess in order to gather information.

As a business owner, you should be asking questions all day long of everyone with whom you interact. Ask questions of your employees, clients, vendors, partners, and competitors. Ask about their experiences. Ask directly what is working and what is not. What can be done different? Better? Faster? Cheaper? More efficiently?

Asking questions is especially critical for marketing and sales efforts. You have most likely answered hundreds and possibly thousands of telemarketing calls thus far in your life. Have you noticed the difference between those sales individuals who begin talking immediately, who go on and on, endlessly spouting off the features or benefits of their service and who don't allow you to get a word in edgewise, versus those who immediately begin the call by asking questions?

Sales Scripts

I have a tremendous amount of respect and patience for individuals who show they value my thoughts, opinions, and insights and who reveal this by asking questions. It surprises me, however, how few sales professionals truly understand the power of questions. Nothing is more irritating than answering the phone and having someone go off on a five-minute verbal barrage. It is as if they are afraid to allow the customer to speak. Yet, ironically, they are going to receive exactly what they fear the most: rejection. If you fail to ask questions in a sales-oriented environment, the foundation is set for failure. Consider the following conversation that I participated in earlier this morning. The phone rang, and I answered.

"Hello, is Mr. Warnock there?"

"This is he," I responded.

"My name is James," said the individual on the line. "I am not calling to sell you anything today. I am with XYZ Financial. As you may know, interest rates have declined considerably. This presents an incredible opportunity for you to refinance your mortgage. Our call today is free and gives you the opportunity to talk to one of our loan refinance specialists at no cost. We have the most experienced, best trained, and proven originators in the nation. We have been around since 1920 and specialize in residential refinances. Please hold, and you will be connected to one of our residential loan specialists."

As I patiently waited for this sales person to pause for just a moment, I kept thinking how much more enjoyable and successful he would be if he simply changed his conversation to a more conversational, relationally oriented script. Consider for a moment what this sales person was relationally revealing to me. That is, what was the above-mentioned sales person telling me about how he saw me in relation to him? It is interesting to see conversations from a relational perspective rather than our traditional informative perspective, isn't it? Relationally, this sales person was revealing to me that I was not personally important to him; I was merely a number, a sales prospect, one of hundreds that he would likely speak with today. Does this make me, as a participant in this exchange, feel valued, cared for, or important? Of course not.

Consider the difference between the traditional, linear, impersonal exchange that occurred as related above to the following personal, question-based, relationally oriented exchange that I propose below:

"Hello, is Mr. Warnock there?"

"My name is James. Do you have a moment to talk, or should I call you back at a better time?"

"I'm with XYZ Financial. I'm sure you have heard that interest rates were cut dramatically last week?"

"My records show that your present interest rate is above 7 percent—does that sound correct?"

"Are you familiar with our no-cost refinancing program?"

"Would you be interested in talking to a refinance specialist about your money-saving options? There is no obligation, and it is free. May I connect you now?"

Both scripts accomplish the same objective. There is an introduction, orientation, and call to action, yet one uses questions to involve the homeowner and one only lectures. One invites participation from the outset, the other passivity. One provides freedom of choice, the other offers no choice. One values the homeowner personally and relationally, the other hopes for inaction and assumes that no response is a positive result. Which conversation would you prefer? Which script do you feel would be most successful?

Questions are a valuable tool. The ability to ask questions is your greatest asset. Get into the habit now of constantly asking questions and really listening to the answers.

Take customer service, for example. Empower your customer service representatives by teaching them to ask questions. Asking questions is empowering. When you ask questions, you have not offered any promises. You have not revealed any secrets. You have not promised any particular result. Asking questions, in terms of our human highways, is simply looking over your shoulder to check the blind spot before changing lanes. Asking questions provides you with the opportunity to gather information. It does not make you any less free in terms of your next choice of action; if anything, it provides you with a wealth of opportunities that did not exist previously.

In driving, looking in your blind spots will save you and your passengers' lives. Similarly, training yourself, your managers, and all your employees to ask questions first will save your business's life. Asking questions should be not only the main way your employees are taught to interact with customers, it should also be the main tool employed to successfully manage and train employees. Lead by example.

Preoccupied Sales Clerk

Imagine that you are the owner or manager of a retail store. You have established a store policy that all customers must be acknowledged and greeted upon entering. You have a particular sales clerk who often does not notice or acknowledge customers as they enter the store. What do you do? How do you approach this situation? You have innumerable options at your disposal. You can ignore the issue. You can show your irritation with the employee nonverbally or verbally. You can terminate the employee. You can threaten. You can subtly beat around the bush by sharing with this particular employee how proud or appreciative you are of another employee who does greet every customer. The list goes on. However, let's say that overall you do appreciate this employee and would like to retain and retrain him or her. You determine that the best option is to talk openly and directly with the employee about this unacceptable behavior. So you arrange an appropriate time, ask the employee into your office, and then begin the conversation. Suppose you began by saying the following:

"I noticed today that when a customer entered the store, you did not follow company procedure and acknowledge or greet them. This is unacceptable."

Notice how many assumptions are embedded in these two beginning sentences. You are assuming that the employee noticed the customer enter. You assume that the employee knew the expectations. You assume there is no good reason for the employee's behavior. Now, you may indeed have facts validating these assumptions, but the point being made here is that when you make fact-based statements rather than asking questions, you share relationally with the other person that you have all the information needed to properly judge and correct them. You have disempowered them. You offer them no space to alter, impact, or change how they are being viewed. On a relational level, you are telling them that the way you see the world is the way the world is. You are relationally emphasizing that you are the boss, the authority, that you possess all the control in the relationship, and that their opinions, values, and attitudes are of little value.

Compare, however, the traditional authority-based training conversation above with the following question-based conversation:

"I observed a customer come into the store today when you were working the floor, and I have a slight concern. Would you feel comfortable if we talked about this for a moment?"

"Do you know which customer I am specifically referring to?"

"Did you notice the customer enter the store?"

"May I ask what caused the delay in greeting the customer?"

"You are familiar with our store policy to greet every customer immediately upon entering, correct?"

"Is there something you possibly could have done differently to ensure the customer was greeted when they entered?"

"Is there anything we as a management team can do to help you in making sure that this policy is adhered to in the future?"

"Do you have any other concerns or questions that I can answer about this or any other issue?"

"I appreciate you taking time and talking with me today. I hope you know how much I value and appreciate you. I have noticed how great you are at merchandising."

So, if you were the employee in the above scenario, which

training procedure would you prefer? Why? As a business owner or manager, always remember that the most effective way to avoid making assumptions is by asking open-ended questions. By asking questions, you are gathering facts before forming opinions, making judgments, or taking action. Interestingly, often the simple practice of asking questions will correct the behavior without any further action having to be taken. By asking the above questions, you are retraining an employee without judgment or criticism. You are simply asking for clarification and understanding while simultaneously reemphasizing your expectations.

It is important to note that in the first claim-based training scenario, you relationally revealed to the other that you do not personally care much for the employee, whether this was your intention or not. Relationally, you were revealing to the employee that the customer is more important than him or her. However, by asking questions of the employee, you reveal that you equally value him or her, as the employee, and the customer.

Begin today by asking questions—of everyone, everywhere, and in every situation. Similar to filling a need, asking questions is something you can begin doing immediately. A muscle is strengthened through use. Before entering into conversations with customers, write down viable questions you can ask. Similarly, before engaging an employee in training, write down a few questions you can ask rather than statements you can make. Do the same with vendors, suppliers, managers, partners, and everyone with whom you interact. It is important to realize that anything you say can be said more powerfully, and with less assumptive risk, by asking a question.

If you consistently focus on the power of questions in your interpersonal relationships, you will soon find yourself thinking of questions to ask rather than making statements and judgments during all of your interactions. By employing this Success Tip alone, you can powerfully change both your professional and your personal world.

SUCCESS TIP #6
ASK QUESTIONS!

SUCCESS TIP #7

WHO TO TRUST?

> "Use your own good judgment in all situations. There will be no additional rules."
>
> Bruce, Jim, and John Nordstrom
> Employee Handbook, Nordstrom Department Store
>
> "Trust yourself. You know more than you think you do."
>
> Benjamin Spock
> Pediatrician and Author

IN 2003, MY WIFE and I were nominated as finalists for the annual Ernst & Young Entrepreneur of the Year award. Warnock's Inc. (DBA Landvoice) had doubled in revenues, subscribers, and net income every year since its inception in 1990. The numbers were impressive, yet I felt we had just tapped the tip of the iceberg. One of the more popular and well-known judges for the program became interested in our business. He commented that in all his years of judging the Entrepreneur of the Year award, he had not seen financials quite as impressive as ours. We began talking. This individual was well known and accomplished in the local business community. It was with a sense of pride that I signed a comprehensive consulting contract with this individual. I was proud to have someone of his caliber now involved in our operations. I intended to follow this individual's counsel closely. I learned a great lesson from this experience.

This consulting contract commenced five years ago. The last five years have been a nightmare. It started with his suggestion that the company needed new people. We brought in new accountants, new sales people, new managers, and new programmers. With new people came new processes. We began revamping our accounting policies, implementing new sales and marketing strategies, and writing new software programs. The results were astonishing—in not such a great way. The new president who took over my position was inexperienced, in over his head, and completely ineffectual. As I referred to earlier, loyal, reliable, committed, and long-time employees were terminated. Lawsuits with some of these former employees were instigated. Company expenses increased at an alarming rate. Taxes were not paid. Accounting fraud occurred, which took years to uncover. Gross and net revenues declined significantly.

Thirteen years of building a successful and immensely profitable enterprise, and it took less than eighteen months to fly it into the ground. I am not blaming others for these failures. I take full responsibility for the decisions made. I am simply sharing my experience in hopes of helping you avoid some of the same mistakes. The question is, how did such a disaster occur, and how can you avoid a similar catastrophe?

The answer is astonishingly simple. I did not adhere strictly to Success Tip #7. I put my trust in others above myself. I believed that others' suggestions were more valuable than my own thoughts. I often wonder why I placed so much trust in outside consultants. I have concluded that I trusted others so intently for one reason: they were not me. Isn't it interesting that when we deem someone more successful, wealthier, better connected, or more experienced than us, we seem to trust their opinions above our own? I clearly let other opinions and suggestions carry more weight than my own. I assumed that because of their credentials, experience, and résumés, they had better business sense than I did. Another invaluable lesson learned.

You know your business better than anyone. You know your employees, customers, partners, vendors, and product or service better than anyone else. You know the pulse of the business environment. You feel it. You live it. Never allow an outside consultant, expert, or so-called guru let you feel he knows more about your business than you do. Trust yourself above all others—always.

The good news is that I was able to resuscitate Landvoice by realigning the company with our original history. We distanced ourselves from unproductive outside consultants and returned to prior and successful internal systems, processes, and values. There is power and relevance in Ralph Waldo Emerson's famous statement from his essay on self-reliance: "Trust thyself: every heart vibrates to that iron string."[1]

At the outset of starting your business, it is important to understand that you are just as wise, just as smart, and just as knowledgeable as anybody else. In fact, you know more, feel more, and understand more about your particular business than any other business professional, regardless of his credentials.

Over the years, I've invested hundreds of thousands of dollars to retain the services of high profile marketing companies, successful public relations firms, accounting professionals, and highly connected business consultants. Many of these professional service companies and consultants came highly recommended, had incredible credentials and successful histories, and provided powerful testimonials. Having the ability to hire such accomplished consultants, it seemed to be a no-brainer. To think that I could have such experience and strength working on my behalf to further my objectives was exciting.

I went through a stage in my entrepreneurial career in which I believed these consulting companies were wiser, smarter, more experienced, and more in touch with current business conditions than I was. As a result, I accepted their advice and suggestions with complete trust and few questions. I paid them tens of thousands of dollars for various campaigns and strategies. Some of the ideas they suggested I disagreed with. Certain suggestions they made just did not feel quite right. However, remembering that these consultants had been around the block a few times, I determined that they must know what they are doing, so I consented. It was a difficult lesson for me to learn. Without exception, every time I choose to follow another's advice that went against my own initial thoughts, judgments, values, and common sense, I live to regret it. This Success Tip, "Trust Yourself above All Others—Always," is mandatory for business success. This important Success Tip can be stated in any number of ways: stand firm, trust your own judgment, and be critical and slow to act.

Let's be clear on what I am and what I am not saying. I am not saying that you should never engage others in your business. I am not saying that you should never trust others' opinions or that you should not seek outside advice, counsel, and so forth. Indeed, there are definitely times to seek professional counsel, professional services, advisors, attorneys, and consultants. Listen to them. Counsel with them. Ask questions of them. Involve them. Yet never, ever, ever allow yourself to be influenced in making decisions with which you are not 100 percent comfortable. Never trust anyone above yourself. When in doubt, follow your gut! As I often remind my children when they are facing important decisions, feel the answer, don't think it! Your body feels more than your mind can comprehend.

You may retain consultants and advisors who suggest actions based on strategies that you might have difficulty fully understanding. This difficulty may result because of the complexity or newness of the strategy or your lack of experience with new strategies. These highly trusted consultants or advisors may even say something to the effect of "Trust me, I have seen this work wonderfully before. You won't regret it." However, I admonish you, when you do not fully understand a strategy or suggestion, are not clear about it, or are not comfortable with it, just say no! It is your business. You make the decisions.

No one cares for the business the way you care. No one knows the business as you know it. No one is as connected to the employees, the customers, the vendors, the environment, and the nuances of your business as you. At times you may be tempted to dismiss this Success Tip by arguing that you don't have a logical argument that supports your reasoning to reject a specific proposed strategy. You do not need a logical reason. It is your business. Follow your own feelings and no one else's. Never allow anyone to persuade you to make a decision with which you are not completely comfortable. I am reminded of what Warren Buffet said: "Never invest in a business you cannot understand."[2] This is just as true for ideas, strategies, and advice as well.

SUCCESS TIP #7
TRUST YOURSELF ABOVE ALL OTHERS—ALWAYS!

Notes

1. Ralph Waldo Emerson, *Essays: First Series* (n.p., 1841), 6.
2. Siimon Reynolds, comp., *Thoughts of Chairman Buffett: Thirty Years of Unconventional Wisdom from the Sage of Omaha* (New York: HarperBusiness, 2008).

SUCCESS TIP #8
WHAT'S A GATEKEEPER?

COLLABORATING WITH GATEKEEPERS IS one of the most important marketing strategies you can engage in to grow your business. What is a gatekeeper? There are gatekeepers in every industry. Regardless of whether your business deals primarily with a product or a service, retail or wholesale, industrial or commercial, there are gatekeepers in your business arena.

Gatekeepers are those individuals, entities, or companies that have the attention and ears of your audience. They are the established, powerful voices that your potential clients are listening to. Great gatekeepers are those that have been established for a time and have a following and respectability in the arena. Two personal examples will help illustrate.

Landvoice Gatekeepers

Our real estate company did well for the first three years. Gross revenues grew by about 50 percent each year. In these early days, direct sales was not only our primary but also our only marketing strategy. And it worked fairly well. Over those first few years, word of mouth kept spreading. Soon we had the attention of some of the industry's top real estate coaches and training organizations. Only after negotiating a partnership agreement with some of these organizations did I fully understand the incredible value that gatekeepers can bring to a small company. When these well-known organizations began promoting our service, our phones nearly immediately began ringing off the hook. We were swamped in a sea of requests that boggled our minds. Gross revenues tripled for the next several years.

Sweet & Sassy Gatekeepers

Similarly, when we first opened Sweet & Sassy, we immediately began asking and observing whom the girls—and their parents—were listening to. We discovered that Miley Cyrus (aka Hannah Montana), Radio Disney, and Disney Network were powerful gatekeepers for this particular audience. These girls were watching Hannah Montana on TV, listening to her music, attending her concerts, and even dressing, acting, and eating like her.

In addition, we discovered that young girls and their parents were investing a lot of their time and energy into extracurricular activities like sports, dance, and gymnastics.

Because of our findings, we immediately established partnerships with these gatekeepers. We ran commercials on Disney Radio and TV. We promoted limo rides and tickets to Hannah Montana concerts. We held Hannah Montana karaoke contests. We contacted nearly every dance and gymnastic academy in the local area, establishing birthday specials and promoting combined marketing events, monthly guest speakers, and annual karaoke contests. It worked wonders. Just two months into business, we were generating more parties and party-related revenue than any other franchise in the country.

Creating Your Gatekeeper List

When creating these lucrative and invaluable gatekeeper relationships, first make a list of potential gatekeepers with whom you could collaborate. This can be done by following a simple three-step process.

Step one: Specifically define your ideal customer.

Step two: Research how your typical clients spend their time and energy.

Step three: Identify the gatekeepers.

Step One—Define Your Customer

Begin making a list of potential gatekeepers by first specifically defining your primary and ideal customers. Do not take this step lightly. If you are opening a restaurant, for example, it may be tempting to say that your ideal customer is everyone who eats and has a credit card with an available balance. This is faulty logic. You simply do not serve everyone equally. What kinds of food do you serve? What are your specialties? What particular age group will feel comfortable in your establishment? Who is browsing your website? Similarly, ensure that you consider how variables such as income, religious affiliation, and political, social, cultural, economic, and professional demographics influence your clients. In sum, ensure you're answering the question of who seems to be most interested in your products or services and why. Clearly thinking through and writing down your ideal clients is an invaluable exercise.

Step Two—Research How Your Typical Clients Spend Their Time and Energy

There are hundreds of thousands of companies in the country that specialize in market research. Do a Google search of marketing consultants and marketing research firms in your state and the number of results will surprise you. Some of these firms may prove helpful. However, in most cases, hiring these firms is simply not necessary. You can obtain similar information with simple conversations. It is amazing how powerful the art of asking questions is.

Years ago, just after starting Landvoice, I was on the phone with a client. She mentioned that she had just returned from a real estate conference in California. Rather than dismiss this information, I immediately began asking questions. What was the conference about? Who spoke? How many were in attendance? How long had she been a member? What was the name of the conference? Did she attend other conferences? This twenty-minute conversation proved to be a game changer.

First, this simple conversation cemented a lifelong

friendship with one of the top real estate agents in the country. To this day, we continue to talk and she remains one of the company's most loyal customers. More importantly, this conversation yielded the names of several top real estate training organizations with which I was unfamiliar. Eventually we were able to partner with two of these organizations. They have since grown into our largest affiliate partners (gatekeepers) and presently generate hundreds of thousands of dollars of revenue every month. All of this was a direct result of this original spontaneous conversation.

You will acquire helpful information through everyday conversations. As you converse with your customers, take special note of companies, entities, and individuals who are role models, celebrities, trainers, educators, coaches, and teachers in your industry. Also, pay particular attention to professional organizations, associations, schools, and governmental licensing and certification departments that serve your clients. Additionally, it is important to discover which conventions, events, shows, and activities your particular customers attend. Do not be afraid to show interest in your clients. Ask directly what they are involved in, what they like, and how they spend their time. Asking questions of your clients and potential clients as you interact with them not only solidifies relationships but will also yield treasures of knowledge.

Below is a partial list of questions you could consider asking your clients:

1. What professional associations and organizations do you belong to?
2. What educational and certificate programs or schools do you participate in?
3. What clubs, groups, and organizations are you involved with?
4. What was the last event, convention, or training forum you attended?

5. Do you have a coach, trainer, or mentor who has been influential in your life?
6. Whom would you consider a role model?
7. What are your favorite TV programs?
8. What magazines and newspapers do you read?
9. What is your favorite music?
10. What is your favorite restaurant?
11. What radio stations do you listen to most?
12. Who are your favorite musical artists?
13. Which celebrities do you pay most attention to?
14. Where do you most like to vacation?
15. How do you spend your free time?
16. What do you do for fun?
17. What is one of your greatest professional accomplishments?
18. Were you professionally recognized for this accomplishment? If so, when and how?

Did you notice how the above questions were organized? The first six questions are focused on asking about your client's academic and professional organizations. The next group of questions is oriented toward your customer's use of the media and arts. The final group of questions deals with leisure activities, vacations, and free time. There is nothing sacred about asking these specific questions. They are provided to get you started. Feel free to make up your own. Their value lies in your willingness to begin talking to, researching, and learning about your customers. In this process, you are simultaneously gathering critical marketing information.

At first, you may feel self-conscious about asking such personal questions. You may think you are being intrusive. I have discovered that honesty alleviates nearly all concerns. Ask them candidly up front, "May I ask you a few questions?" Tell them precisely what you are doing: attempting to understand the market better. These conversations will not only deepen your understanding of the marketplace, but you will also gain the trust and respect of the customers with whom you converse. Everybody loves being treated like somebody.

Step Three—Determine the Real Gatekeepers

Notice in my earlier example that upon discovering that Hannah Montana was a gatekeeper, I did not attempt to call her directly. That is simply not necessary. The first step is to determine *how* your customers interact with each particular gatekeeper. The real gatekeepers are the people and places where your customers actually encounter the gatekeeper. For example, in the case of Hannah Montana, our clients were not interacting with her personally; rather they were listening to her music, watching her movies and TV shows, and attending her concerts. The real gatekeepers for Hannah Montana were the radio stations, TV stations, and concert venues promoting her shows.

Once you have identified who the real gatekeepers are, you will need to contact them personally. Gatekeepers became gatekeepers by knowing the industry. They are open to new ideas, products, and services. You will find, as I have, that the vast majority of gatekeepers are inherently interested in what you are doing to meet the needs of the marketplace. They did not become gatekeepers in their industry by burying their heads in the sand. On the whole, they are approachable.

The irony is that because most business owners are not willing to do the hard work themselves, few of these gatekeepers will have had direct contact with the actual owners of businesses. Being personally involved will allow you to begin conversations that could have long-lasting benefits for both of you. It is also relatively easy as an owner of a company to get in doors often shut to others. Introducing yourself as the owner and founder of a particular company carries a weight that is understood and respected. Even if you find that some of these gatekeepers are already in partnership with a competitor, at the very least, you are afforded the chance to introduce yourself and the advantages of your product and service compared to the competition. You have left the door open for possible future relationships.

Why Gatekeepers Are Essential

There are at least four critical reasons why gatekeepers should be a central component of your ongoing marketing strategy.

First, collaborating with gatekeepers provides you with an immediate audience. Gatekeepers have well-established and ongoing communication with their customers, followers, vendors, and the marketplace in general. In collaborating with a gatekeeper, you gain the attention of the same audience. It has likely taken years for the gatekeeper to establish a voice in the marketplace and create a following. By collaborating with them, you immediately tap into an enormous pool of potential clients.

Second, collaborating with gatekeepers gives you immediate credibility. Gatekeepers are generally well-known in the industry. People respect and trust their opinions and advice. I have always believed that testimonial advertising is the most important and effective marketing achieved. Working closely with gatekeepers allows you to effectively multiply testimonial marketing tactics with the voice of a respected coach, trainer, vendor, or celebrity in the industry. The summed results can be staggering.

As I alluded to earlier, I remember vividly the day that my real estate data company finalized a partnership with a well-known industry magazine. The first day they mentioned our services in their publication, our phones did not stop ringing for days. By the time we had answered a call and signed up a new subscriber, there were twenty more new messages waiting. Such results will bring huge grins on owners' faces. It was as if a floodgate had been opened. Gatekeepers are called gatekeepers for a reason.

Third, collaborating with a gatekeeper is inexpensive.

Notice throughout this chapter that I use the word partnership. A partnership implies dual interests. It suggests shared ownership. Some gatekeepers will expect you to pay an up-front fee for their services. Magazines, newspapers, radio and TV stations, and billboards are typical gatekeepers that charge a set and structured fee for their services. At times, it may be necessary to pay the standard advertising fees. However, in keeping with Success Tip #3, "Start Simple and Inexpensive," your most valuable gatekeeper relationships will be those created as a partnership, meaning shared ownership. These are the most effective marketing agreements either partner can engage in.

A revenue-sharing partnership with gatekeepers, if structured correctly, is the most cost-effective advertising you can do. An ideal win-win partnership agreement is structured such that the gatekeeper receives a percentage of all gross sales created through their channel. This serves both of your interests well. By paying only on revenues received, you pay only *after* you collect revenues. It is risk-free advertising. If your partner does not do anything or there is little or no response to a message, you pay little or nothing yet still receive exposure.

In traditional advertising (magazines, newspapers, TV and radio spots, bulk mailing, billboards, and so on), you pay to have your message delivered regardless of the results. In these cases, you as the advertiser assume full risk. In a gatekeeper relationship, however, you only pay when you are paid. Setting up a percentage split ensures that your partner has a stake in the outcome. On too many occasions, I was persuaded to sponsor or pay a set fee to supposedly establish a gatekeeper partnership. Nearly always, I have walked away from such situations frustrated and dejected. Sponsoring some event or paying a set fee for your involvement is a one-sided, win-lose arrangement. In these situations, the gatekeeper wins. They receive their compensation immediately and initially. They have no incentive to help you succeed. To ensure a fair and satisfying result for both parties, ensure that you align the gatekeeper's compensation with a percentage of gross revenues generated.

You may be wondering why gatekeepers are interested in forming a partnership at all. After all, why would they be interested in promoting your product or service for a percentage of revenues rather than simply demanding a set advertising fee up front?

Gatekeepers are business oriented. They understand business. They understand the risks inherent in business. They enjoy the gamble. The risks and the rewards entice all of us into business in the first place. Gatekeepers clearly understand the potential rewards. I have established several gatekeeper relationships in my real estate company where we pay specific gatekeepers in excess of $20,000-plus per month in partnership commissions. Had we established typical advertising fees for these partners, their monthly revenue would have been nowhere near this amount. They took a risk and reaped the rewards. As a result, both partners triumphed in true win-win fashion. As you approach and propose partnerships with potential gatekeepers, it is imperative that you speak their language—the language of risk and reward.

And the fourth important reason to partner with gatekeepers is that collaborating with gatekeepers creates an impressive domino effect. You have most likely experienced the joy of seeing and hearing a long line of dominos remain in motion for some time after tipping over a single piece. A primary reason this effect is enjoyed is the notion that it all originated with one single, simple action. Thus it is in business as well. Dominoes is a perfect metaphor representing exactly what happens when an effective gatekeeper relationship is structured. First, the domino effect works within each gatekeeper organization. It is important for you to realize that the most difficult work you will engage in with all gatekeepers is getting that first sale. Toppling the first domino will require effort. You may spend countless hours on the phone with gatekeepers describing your services, proposing structures, negotiating details, writing up proposals, reviewing counter proposals, and so on. Typically, you do all of this before you ever see the first domino fall. As discussed in Success Tip #4, you as the business owner should, at least initially, plan on doing this hard work yourself. Once you have personally contacted, negotiated, signed up, and successfully initiated the partnership process with several gatekeepers and have recorded the process in your operational journal, it then may be appropriate to hand off this task to another.

However, once you get that first domino in motion—the first announcement made to the gatekeeper's audience—the process becomes easy and repetitive. Just like in dominoes, once the gatekeeper experiences a few positive sales and they receive their first commission check, they understand the potential. You will find these gatekeepers begin sharing your story everywhere at an ever-increasing rate. You may find yourself stunned by the long-term positive effects of one simple gatekeeper partnership.

The domino effect is not limited to one particular collaborator, however. The domino effect actually occurs on multiple levels. Just like in dominoes, gatekeepers are situated closely to each other. Other gatekeepers whom you do not know or whom you have not yet contacted will become familiar with your products and services. This awareness not only further confirms your legitimacy in the marketplace but also enables you to create additional partnerships at a more accelerated rate. The effects of one domino set in motion can have far-reaching effects in multiple directions and across multiple industries.

SUCCESS TIP #8
PARTNER WITH GATEKEEPERS!

SUCCESS TIP #9
EVERYONE? ALWAYS? REGARDLESS?

Sweet & Sassy—Paid Time Off (PTO)

In 2007, we sold the franchise rights for Sweet & Sassy in Utah. About a month before the expected sale, several employees approached me about a concern with the lack of paid time off (PTO) benefits. This was a difficult request. The store had not earned money since its inception. To continue operating, I found it necessary to feed the store out of the profits of my other enterprises. Yet I knew I was also less than a month away from potentially selling the business. The last thing I wanted was to rock the ship and risk losing vital employees just before closing the sale. I chose a delay tactic. I indicated to the employees that I would be willing to discuss the issue in more detail in a month.

In reality, I was hoping that I would have the business sold and the new owners could deal with the issue. As often happens, the sale was delayed, and I found myself with employees demanding a response to the PTO issue. I begrudgingly worked up a solution, offering limited PTO hours but silently hoping that the sale would go through before any PTO requests were made.

The sale did close, and I was free . . . or so I thought. I successfully avoided paying any PTO prior to the sale. It was now the new owner's responsibility, right? Wrong. It came as a total surprise to the new owners when the first request for PTO was made based on the agreement I had drafted just weeks before closing. The new owners, surprised by the request, contacted me for clarification. I was stuck.

I had closed the sale without appropriately identifying and crediting this possible liability to the new owners. Initially I wanted to fight this unexpected liability and spent a few days discussing options with attorneys. I soon realized that the cost of representation would cost as much—if not more—than the PTO liabilities. I ultimately ended up compensating the buyers for all the employees PTO hours. How I wish I had been honest and upright not only with the new owners, but also initially with the employees. Though it was not appropriate to inform the employees of the potential future sale of the store, it would have been best to be up front and honest with the employees about the present financial concerns. I should have indicated that the store was not generating sufficient revenues to warrant PTO benefits at that time and that such a request could be addressed in the future, but with no promises. I could have—and should have—been honest with the employees and allowed the cards to fall where they may.

I also should have been up front and honest with the buyers of the store. It is interesting how easy it is in the heat of the moment to withhold information and paint a slightly different picture of reality to ensure that a desired deal, agreement, sale, or event occurs. It is in these moments that you must stand up for what is right and honest—regardless.

Oftentimes the easiest way to do this is to take a long-term perspective. Often, hiding or withholding the truth is a short-term solution for a long-term issue. By looking beyond the immediate situation and envisioning a year or two further down the road, you will see more clearly that absolute honesty, regardless of the situation, is always the best policy.

Landvoice—Sales Commissions

In 2004, real estate was booming nationwide. Sales at Landvoice followed the trend. We had just finished 2003 with both net and gross revenues far exceeding expectations. I had an excellent sales, accounting, and customer support staff. In the midst of this success, my accounting department brought to my attention that I was not being honest to myself. At the time, I was writing some very large monthly commission payments to internal sales employees and outside gatekeeper affiliates.

My accountant indicated that I was paying those commission checks after I paid the credit card processing fees. My accountant reminded me that it was within my contractual rights to ask employees and partners to share in these expenses. It made perfect sense to me. It seemed only fair that my sales personnel and my gatekeeper partners should share such processing expenses. I immediately implemented a change to the calculations for all commissions. I did this, however, without communicating such a change to either the employees or the partners.

Not surprisingly, a few weeks later the water hit the fan. My employees and partners began receiving their commission checks with a small but significant deduction. Immediately I had a stampede of unhappy sales people at my door. I was shocked by the response. In hindsight, I wonder why I was so shocked. After all, I was playing with people's paychecks.

Eventually, my loyal sales manager inquired about his own reduced check. I tried to explain the reasons, but in hindsight, my explanations were self-serving and defensive. He left my office flustered and agitated.

I justified my actions by explaining that I was only being fair with myself. Selfish thoughts, at the time, kept me from realizing my mistake. I simply should have communicated with all involved parties, honestly and openly, well in advance of payday, about my concerns. Honest and straightforward communication could have easily resolved this issue equitably for all parties.

Lack of honest communication eventually led to the disintegration of a very effective sales team. In a very short time, I received several resignations from some of my top sales people. A few weeks later, my trusted and valuable sales manager approached me with a desire to work on a different project closer to home. I was actually relieved. The tension arising from this sales commission fiasco had made it somewhat uncomfortable for us to continue working together. I signed an agreement making this possible.

A few weeks later, I was informed that my former sales manager was inappropriately communicating with some of my most valued business partners. I presented the accusations to him, and tensions grew quickly. In an attempt to defend my company, I retained counsel and filed a lawsuit. What had been a successful relationship just a few weeks earlier had turned sour fast. It all began with a subtle but real lack of honest communication with my sales team.

Unfortunately, the story does not end there. Not long after filing a legal suit, seeking to stop said sales manager from inappropriately contacting my business partners, I faced a difficult decision. It stated, in the departure contract that I signed, that I would provide a ninety-day notice of cancellation. According to the contract, I was to continue to pay this former sales manager his earned commissions through this ninety days. I debated what to do. Here was a former employee who I felt was now being dishonest with me. It just did not seem fair paying significant commissions to an individual who was not honest in return.

In counseling with my attorneys and other consultants, I was advised that it might be appropriate to withhold those commissions pending settlement of the lawsuit. At the time, I had a strong feeling that I should pay those commissions as agreed. However, under the stress of the situation, I chose to ignore the rule of complete honesty—always—regardless—and decided not to pay the agreed upon commissions. This decision cost me dearly. It provided the rationale for a counter suit. It led to over two years and hundreds of thousands of dollars in legal fees. It led to countless hours of wasted time both defending and engaging in legal maneuvering. It led to many sleepless nights and endless internal turmoil. With the emotional life sucked out of me, I eventually contacted my former sales manager and agreed to pay those ninety days of commissions if he agreed to drop the lawsuit.

Five years later, I still feel the effect of my errors. My former employee started a competing company providing the exact same service. Now I have several aggressive competitors in the marketplace, all of whom learned the business from me. It all occurred because of my failure to communicate openly and honestly about my feelings and concerns before making decisions and taking action.

I did learn from this mistake, however. I hired a new management team who worked tirelessly alongside me to regain our strong financial footing. I rewarded those who proved themselves with generous profit-sharing incentives. Many of these valuable managers are still with the company to this day.

We often hear how important honesty is. Absolute honesty is essential for business success. Honesty with your employees, partners, investors, and clients is critical. Such honesty extends beyond financial dealings. Honesty is essential in all your actions, your conversations, your training, your discipline, and your promises.

As a small business owner, it is easy to find yourself in a position where everyone needs something from you. Your employees need more money, higher wages, benefits, insurance, paid time off, and flexible hours. Your clients need products or services delivered immediately, with the highest quality and at the lowest price. Your business partners and investors need returns on their investments. They need to know they are heard and require constant communication. It may be impossible to fill all needs all the time. It is possible, however, for you to fill everyone's most important need all of the time. That need is the need for honest and straightforward communication.

Honesty is the most important need that any of your employees, clients, partners, gatekeepers, and investors possess. It is tempting to overpromise a client, delay responding to an employee, and withhold subtle information from an investor. Yet such subtle communication tricks do not help, but will rather hurt your business in the long run. The important point is to state clearly, directly, specifically, and unequivocally exactly what you are willing and able to do—and what you are not willing or able to do.

This rule, treating everyone completely honest, always, and regardless, leads directly to the next Success Tip, "Be Crystal Clear with Contracts." Regardless of whether you are making verbal or written, explicit or implied agreements, always honor exactly what you have agreed to. The secret, however, is to never say, do, or agree to anything unless you are completely prepared to honor it—period!

SUCCESS TIP #9
TREAT EVERYONE COMPLETELY HONEST— ALWAYS—REGARDLESS!

SUCCESS TIP #10
WHAT DO CRYSTALS HAVE TO DO WITH CONTRACTS?

ONE AFTERNOON, MY LOYAL sales manager discussed in the previous chapter asked if he could speak with me in my office. Upon entering and closing the door, he asked me how I would feel if he started an expired service. An expired service was something we had debated for years. An expired service was complementary data to the present for sale by owner data we compiled. Our clients would find similar value in expired leads.

An expired lead is a property owner who listed their property for sale with a realtor but the property did not sell during the listing period. When the listing period ends, the property listing expires. I was somewhat resistant to the idea because it required the development of different technology than we were using. As discussed previously, however, having had some difficulties in my relationship with him, it seemed like a reasonable way to separate amicably. I told him I would support the idea.

The next day he brought in an agreement to sign that clarified our ongoing relationship. I was familiar with the contract, as it was the standard affiliate agreement that we used to work with our gatekeeper partners over the years. I reviewed it to ensure there were no changes. It all seemed clear and straightforward except for one section. I had not noticed the lack of clarity in this particular section. The paragraph read:

"The term of this agreement shall commence on the signature date of this contract and shall terminate 30 days after written notice of cancellation is received by mail or personal delivery. For a period of twelve (12) months after termination of this agreement, Warnock's agrees to maintain service for those client customers who wish to continue Warnock's services. . . ."

This paragraph clearly stated that either party could cancel the agreement with a thirty-day written notice, but it did not clearly state whether earned commissions would need to be paid for thirty days or for the full twelve months after termination. Nowhere in the contract did it clarify this point. We had never run across this issue before, and unfortunately, I failed to demand clarification of this point before signing. I did not want to bring up a point that I did not feel was applicable. I also did not want to rock the boat any more than I had. I was agitated over the whole issue anyway, facing the fact that I was losing a valuable sales manager. I wanted the process finished. I ignored my concerns and signed the agreement.

This decision haunted me. The lawsuit and counter suit described earlier arose because of this lack of clarity in the contract. In hindsight, how I wish I had ensured that every word of the agreement was crystal clear in translation. You will avoid a lot of pain and anguish if you ensure that all agreements are clear.

You may feel pressured, at times, by companies or individuals who you desire to work with but who state that their agreements are non-negotiable. If there is some part of an agreement that you are uncomfortable with—for any reason—I would strongly suggest you approach the situation carefully. Communicate clearly with the other party about your concerns and offer suggested changes. If necessary, ask your attorney to contact the other party on your behalf. A call from a professional third party often works wonders and introduces flexibility where previously there was none.

If the above strategies prove unsuccessful and you remain uncomfortable about particular sections of the contract, I suggest one final communication to the other party—in writing. In a formal letter of concern, state specifically and unapologetically the exact sections and reasons for your concerns. Indicate that regrettably you are not willing to sign the agreement until the concern is resolved. No matter how much you desire to work with a particular company or individual, never allow yourself to be pressured into signing anything that you are not completely comfortable with.

When managing a business, it is easy to find yourself in situations where you simply do not take time to review every sentence of every agreement that passes over your desk. Most large companies have the benefit and convenience of in-house legal counsel to deal with such matters. As a small business owner, however, you are left to decide and structure which contracts are deserving of an attorney review versus which you should personally review. The issue gets further complicated when you hire managers and offer them authority over contracts. In keeping with Success Tip #4, "Do the Hard Work Yourself— Initially," the task of overseeing and approving any agreement and contract for your business is yours.

It is necessary for you to personally oversee, read, review, negotiate, and sign every contract the business engages in, at least initially. Whether you enjoy this kind of work or not is irrelevant. As the business owner, you are ultimately responsible for all agreements. It is critical to understand that this responsibility is yours whether or not you retain an attorney to review your contracts. You must have complete understanding of the requirements that your business is obligated to fulfill. The benefit of being involved initially is that you slowly create, approve, and accumulate a library of standard legal agreements that can be used by others in your organization at will. Over time, your library of approved agreements is referenced, employed, negotiated, and signed with vendors, partners, clients, and service providers with minimal maintenance. Only negotiated changes to the initial approved agreements are necessary.

The question remains, however, which contracts should you have an attorney review? Most attorneys reading this book will likely unanimously and simultaneously answer "all of them." In an ideal world, a space where you have unlimited time and resources, I would agree. Having your basic, standard, often-used agreements in your approved library of agreements reviewed by a professional is wise counsel. However, let's be practical. If you were to employ an attorney to review every proposed word change to every written agreement and contract you engage in as a business owner, you would soon find yourself bankrupt and needing to work for someone else to pay your legal fees.

Contract Specifics

Over the years, and through many personal experiences, I have found a few basic rules that, if followed, will help alleviate many of the legal issues that may arise.

Before signing any agreement, ask yourself the following simple questions:

1. What is the objective and intent of the agreement or contract?
2. What obligations am I under, both explicitly and implied?
3. Am I willing and able to fulfill every obligation outlined?
4. How long is the term of the agreement?
5. Under what circumstances can each party terminate the agreement?
6. After termination, what obligations is each party under and for how long?

Crystal Clear

I purposefully use the word "crystal" in reference to this Success Tip. In its simplest form, a crystal is any natural material that is solid and well-defined, with pleasing geometric shapes. This simple definition of a crystal can be an effective guide to help analyze every agreement and contract you sign.

Each agreement should be *solid*, meaning that it is thorough, complete, and addresses all possible scenarios that may occur in the future.

Similarly, ensure that your agreements are *well-defined*. "Well-defined" refers to the notion that every word of the agreement is clear and comprehensible. There should be no guesswork, unclear elements, or confusing language. Make it simple. Demand simplicity from your attorneys as well.

Finally, each agreement should be *pleasing in shape*. The ultimate objective of any agreement should be the creation of a mutually beneficial arrangement. Any mutually beneficial arrangement should be pleasing to both parties. When you feel unsure, unclear, or uncomfortable with any part of the agreement for any reason, you must communicate your concerns quickly and completely. Do not ever hold back your opinions, thoughts, feelings, concerns, and questions. As has been stated, you, as the owner, are ultimately responsible.

SUCCESS TIP #10
BE CRYSTAL CLEAR WITH CONTRACTS!

SUCCESS TIP #11

SHOULD I RETAKE MATH?

IN THE FALL OF 2006, my wife and I traveled to Dallas, Texas, to view the Sweet & Sassy concept personally. During this visit, I continually asked the franchiser for actual store financials. In every case, I was presented with pro forma numbers. As the term pro forma suggests, the financials provided were not the exact operating finances of the corporate-owned store but rather hypothetical numbers based loosely on previous operations. Being continually rebuffed on getting exact financials (which, of course, should have been a huge red flag), we literally talked ourselves into the business by suggesting that it did not matter what the "real numbers" were anyway. We rationalized that with our unique marketplace, population, and business experience, we were going to hit the ball out of the park regardless of what had previously occurred.

With such self-talk, we invested over a half million dollars creating the largest, most impressive Sweet and Sassy store designed to date. Not once throughout this process did I sit down and analyze anticipated revenues versus expenses in detail. Never did I calculate how many parties and haircuts would be required to pay for the initial investment. I paid little attention to the cost of employees, payroll, health insurance, benefits, taxes, rent, utilities, insurance, shipping, retail supplies, cleaners, and party supplies—all necessary store operations. I functioned off a we-can-make-this-work-regardless attitude. Even as I write this now I shake my head in disbelief. What was I thinking?

It is interesting how often emotions dispel logic. I was so emotionally caught up in the excitement of the enterprise that I did not stop to examine the business's financial feasibility. One year later, I found myself running a retail operation with an average monthly cash deficiency in excess of $20,000. This deficiency occurred while revenues far surpassed projected pro forma revenues. In other words, although we were exceeding estimated gross revenue collections, our monthly expenses were soaring, nearly doubling that of pro forma statements. We changed management. We changed systems. We cut costs. Nothing worked.

As discussed earlier, I made several mistakes in beginning this new venture. First, I ignored two of the most critical Success Tips for starting a new business. I ignored Success Tip #3, "Start Simple and Inexpensive," as well as Success Tip #4, "Do the Hard Work Yourself—Initially." Second, I did not incorporate the present Success Tip, "Know the Numbers." Eventually, out of desperation, I calculated the financial numbers and discovered that in a best-case scenario, we could expect to earn a maximum profit of a few thousand dollars per month. Moreover, this would occur only if I assumed the full-time management duties of the store. In other words, based on accumulated debt and operational expenses, we had dug a hole so deep that it was extremely unlikely we were going to be able to emerge from this pit unscathed. We eventually sold this enterprise and the accompanying franchise rights for a fraction of what we had invested. The good news is that the pain and losses from this failed enterprise could easily have been avoided had I invested a few hours sitting down with a pencil and paper, unemotionally working through the real financial numbers.

It is relevant to mention here why I have placed this Success Tip as Tip #11. As mentioned earlier, I have placed these Success Tips in order of developmental importance. I am convinced that the financial catastrophe of Sweet and Sassy would not have been nearly as significant had I adhered to previous

Success Tips. It is important to realize that knowing the numbers becomes much more relevant to your business only when you begin investing more in your business. In other words, the necessity of knowing the numbers is something that your business grows into and is a direct function of the initial investment required.

When we first began Landvoice, knowing the numbers was very simple. To begin this particular business, our expenses were minimal. Expenses consisted of a phone line, our time, and a fax machine. Initially we decided we would charge $29 a month for client subscription access. We determined we needed a minimum of six clients at $29 a month each (totaling $174 a month) in order to meet expenses and create a nice part-time job, enabling my wife to work at home. Though the numbers were simple, we knew what was needed for success. If you adhere strictly to the Success Tips outlined in this book, you will notice how the value of knowing the numbers will escalate proportionally with your business growth. It is for this reason that I included this Success Tip as one of the final Success Tips.

Mental Monopoly

Knowing the numbers does not mean you need to have an advanced accounting degree or be a wizard at math. Knowing the numbers simply means that you are willing to take the time to sit down and honestly evaluate how the revenues and expenses need to play out in order for the enterprise to operate profitably. You can find a huge library of free financial forms and reports, as well as a host of other valuable financial tools, at www.sba.gov and www.score.org. Regardless of whether you enjoy finances, it will be invaluable for you to take some time and fill out the free monthly income statements provided as a free resource on these websites. After an hour of plugging in hypothetical numbers, you will emerge with an appreciation of what it will take to make your particular business work financially for you. It's nothing more than a mental game of

Monopoly in which you examine the "what ifs" of income and expenses.

As you complete the income statements, I caution you to adhere strictly to Success Tip #9 and be honest with the numbers. It is only natural to try to talk yourself into a potentially great idea that you may be emotionally attached to. However, be honest with yourself. You are the one that will be hurt if you underestimate expenses and exaggerate income. It is a good practice to slightly overestimate all possible expenses.

In sum, investing a little time working through income and expense financials will prove invaluable. The objective of this exercise is not to talk yourself out of the business but rather to ensure that you are going in with your eyes wide open. As a wise sage once said, "You can face the truth initially or you will face it eventually." Once you face the hard, financial numbers and are comfortable with what you see, only then are you truly free to run with the business.

SUCCESS TIP #11
KNOW THE NUMBERS!

SUCCESS TIP #12
WHY WOULD I BOX MY EMPLOYEES?

I HAVE BEEN FORTUNATE to have worked with some extremely talented, dedicated, and valued employees over the past thirty years. I will forever be grateful for many of the wonderful associates who were highly instrumental in the ultimate successes of my businesses. Many of these irreplaceable relationships continue to this day. There is, of course, a balance in all things. Over my entrepreneurial career, I have also lost, fired, or let go dozens of employees. Most of these employees had little overall consequence with the ongoing operations of the business. With the departures of most of these employees, business continued unaffected, and in many cases, the business became more efficient, more profitable, and healthier than before. There have been, however, two or three extremely critical employees over the years who did have a significant and long-term effect on the performance, profitability, and health of the business. When I lost these critical employees, everything changed. The similarities in these critical departures are worth discussing.

Critical Employees

I refer to those rare employees who are immensely valuable and highly motivated as critical employees.

In my experience, critical employees are those with the following characteristics: Typically, they have been with the company for at least two years. They have contributed powerfully in the growth of the business. They have proven themselves incredibly loyal during their employ. Critical employees are intense, motivated, passionate, and highly disciplined. They take pride in their work. You trust them. You have an unusually open and honest relationship with them. You place tremendous value on them.

Unfortunately, I have also learned the following about critical employees. Typically, they quit on their own accord. Often they begin their own business soon after leaving. It is very difficult to replace these critical employees and usually involves lengthy, exhausting, and expensive searches. Later, these critical employees often indicate that the primary reason they left was because they felt *undervalued* and *underappreciated*. I still miss each one of them to this day. In retrospect, I wish I had identified earlier how valuable these few, critical employees were and rewarded them appropriately.

Compensation

Some of the most difficult decisions you face as a business owner involve employee compensation. Employee compensation is a difficult concept. How do you adequately and fairly compensate employees? I would suggest that simply adding one word to the above question will help alleviate many of the typical problems involving employee compensation. Consider the same question with one simple word added:

How do you adequately and fairly compensate *critical* employees?

Earlier, we described critical employees as employees who are both motivated and valued. Consider the two terms. Motivation refers to something inside an individual. It implies a self-driven individual. Motivation is an internal energy that drives a person's actions regardless of outside influences or pressures. Motivation is closely related to passion, as discussed in Success Tip #2.

Value, on the other hand, is an external judgment. It is a possession of an observer. Value implies worth to another.

Undoubtedly, highly valued employees have many strengths, characteristics, gifts, talents, and abilities. Through personal experience, I have come to understand that those individuals who are highly motivated also naturally possess many other characteristics, abilities, strengths, and gifts that make them invaluable. I do not believe it a coincidence that every one of my most valuable employees who left my employ eventually began their own businesses. Why? Because each of them were motivated and passionate individuals. They had the energy, commitment, dedication, pride, power, and ability to accomplish great works. They accomplished great things while they were in my employ and continued to do so after they had left.

There are innumerable leadership and management books written about how to motivate employees. This present work is not an attempt to discuss and describe such motivational techniques. Rather, my intent is to simply share a few valuable lessons and insights I have learned about employee relationships and compensation.

Employee Motivation Rating

I usually resist categorizations. Too often we pigeonhole individuals by drawing arbitrary lines around dissimilar elements. However, for simplicity and ease, the following categorization may be helpful. Employees generally fit into one of four categories:

1. Highly motivated and highly valued employees
2. Less motivated but still valued
3. Highly motivated yet undervalued
4. Unmotivated and of low value

MOTIVATION

	HIGH	LOW
HIGH	Box 1	Box 2
LOW	Box 3	Box 4

V
A
L
U
E

Box One Employees

In an attempt to identify which of your present employees are most valued, categorize each of them using the Employee Motivation Rating. Think of each of your present employees and place the name of each employee in the box you feel is most appropriate. Reserve Box 1 for those few, critical employees who are: 1) highly motivated, 2) highly valued, and 3) essential in maintaining and growing your business.

You recognize Box 1 employees immediately. They are workers. They are dedicated and diligent. If your experience is similar to mine, you will notice how Box 1 employees possess an innate, natural, and internal motivation. They possess a drive and passion that propels and motivates from within. Rarely do you find employees who are only externally motivated listed in Box 1.

Once you categorize each of your employees, look again at those employees you have placed in Box 1. These individuals are worth their weight in gold. Reward them generously, not only financially but also socially, personally, and relationally. In every way possible, let them know and feel how valuable they are. Ensure they know how much you appreciate their efforts. Take notice of their personal lives, dreams, hopes, and activities. Involve yourself in their day-to-day life. Be professional, but also be personal, approachable, and active with these employees. I have found it so easy in the hectic day-to-day issues facing me as a business owner to become impersonal, detached, and reactive. While always honoring professional standards of conduct, it is possible and essential to let these employees know—relationally—how much you value them. One of your primary business objectives must be to do all you can to keep Box 1 employees.

Critical Employee Revenue Sharing (CERS)

Your most valued and motivated employees are also those who may be considering opening a business of their own. Through experience, I now employ a powerful retention strategy involving Critical Employee Revenue Sharing (CERS). It is possible that some reading these words will immediately experience a panicked disbelief that I am proposing such a program. You may be tempted to immediately and completely reject such a concept. Pause to consider the benefits of such a program. Critical employee revenue sharing is a benefit package that allows a small number of your most valued Box 1 employees to participate in a small way with the ongoing profitability and success of your company. The term Critical Employee Revenue Sharing is chosen purposefully. First, the program is limited to your most motivated, trusted, active, and full-time managerial employees. Take special note of the terms "active" and "full-time." You should be clear—in writing—when offering such a benefit so that the employee completely understands that when their employment is suspended, discontinued, or terminated for any reason, so is the revenue sharing benefit. Ensuring the employee also signs a solid non-compete and non-disclosure agreement is mandatory. Obviously, it is wise to consult with an employment attorney on properly structuring the strategy.

Consider for a moment the long-term potential benefits of such a program. When a valued employee is tied into the profitability of the company, they feel ownership. Their instinctive drive to start a business of their own is somewhat satisfied. Often these highly motivated employees did not need further personal motivation, but you will notice how their dedication, energy, passion, and overall concern for the welfare of the company solidify. They walk, talk, and act with a new purpose, a new plan. They become an even more trusted voice of support, counsel, and wisdom in the present and in years to come.

In addition, because you tied revenue sharing into an ongoing employment relationship, you have cemented a long-term relationship. The prospect of this employee leaving for some other opportunity diminishes considerably. Competing companies will find it difficult to match such an offer. Further, the likelihood of this employee jumping ship when he both has a guaranteed salary plus revenue sharing and belongs to an organization where he feels valued and honestly treated is minute.

The CERS program is clearly structured so that the revenue sharing occurs on a very small percentage of net revenues. This ensures that you are sharing profits only after all salaries, rents, taxes, and all other expenses and benefits are paid in full. You have now invited the employee into your central circle. They will share in all that is earned and received. They participate in the financials, debts, lawsuits, wins, and losses. They feel and know that they are highly appreciated, valued, and recognized. The percentage that you share can be very small. Obviously, the percentage you share depends on a host of variables, including past financials, past trends, number of benefit participants, overall historical profitability, and so on. Depending on the size and profitability of your present company, I suggest keeping the revenue sharing percentage somewhere between .5 percent (half of 1 percent) and a maximum of 5 percent.

Motivated employees do not need much to recognize the ultimate value of what you are offering. After initially losing some critically important executives, I retained some outstanding managers and executives using this program. Many of these critical employees I would have lost had it not been for this "share the wealth" benefit.

Box Two Employees

Though this Success Tip focuses on your most valued and motivated (Box 1) employees, there is value in discussing the other types of employees briefly. Those employees that you placed in Box 2 (less motivated but valued) probably represent a majority of your employees. Box 2 employees are there for the paycheck. They are generally willing to do what is called for, but only as requested. They are not particularly ambitious or proactive but typically complete assigned tasks. Though they are valuable, they are also replaceable.

Box Three Employees

The third group of employees are those employees who may be highly motivated, but for a variety of reasons are of lower value. Typically you have more Box 3 employees in larger organizations. Keep a close eye on employees in this category. Often, these employees simply may be in the wrong position. If they are truly motivated, they could become frustrated very quickly with what they deem as a substandard job opportunity. I strongly suggest you consider what other more meaningful opportunities you could offer such employees. They have great potential but need the right opportunity.

Box Four Employees

The fourth group of employees are typically employees who occupy important and vital positions within your organization but are not performing to expectation. When you have an employee in a vital and important position lacking motivation, you notice. You will find yourself constantly wondering exactly what they are accomplishing. You will question their performance. You will wonder what they are doing with their time.

Generally, employees within this category always have

excuses for failures. They often point to other employees, technology, economy, competition, lack of adequate compensation, lack of benefits, or negative features of your product or service as excuses for their lack of success. In my experience, these employees are piranhas. They literally eat away the organization. They take, consume, digest, and rarely give back. If left without intervention, they can suck the lifeblood right out of your organization.

Box 4 employees have mastered the role of being paid for doing very little. Often they appear busy, they seem to be working, yet, in actuality, they are like an empty cup. They have little to show for their efforts. Worse, the substandard performance has a negative impact on the overall culture of the business. Box 4 employees not only prey on excuses, they are also masters of deceit. They are great talkers. They appear to have an effective grasp on every nuance of the business. They have mastered the art of stage presence. They fool their immediate supervisors and managers. They play employees against each other. They are masters at creating subtle, secret combinations of cliques and groups that can tear apart the cohesiveness and teamwork of a company or department.

In my experience, termination, as quick and clean as possible, is the best strategy. However, in a few cases, I have found that a direct, clear, and honest questioning interview, preceding a termination notice, may yield valuable results.

Questioning Interview

In keeping with Success Tip #6, "Ask Questions," the most valuable and risk-free approach to substandard employees is to ask questions. In preparation, I suggest you develop a list of potential questions you will ask before scheduling the interview. As discussed earlier, asking questions is the most important tool you have in managing employees. Asking questions allows you to obtain valuable information without appearing to judge, criticize, or blame. It reveals respect, concern, and value for the employee and their unique situation. I suggest you keep this conversation as informal and relaxed as possible. Here are a few possible questions you might ask employees during this questioning interview:

1. Are you enjoying your work?
2. Is your work schedule fitting with the other demands in your life?
3. What is your favorite part of the job?
4. What is your least favorite part of the job?
5. How do you feel you are performing?
6. Is there something else you would prefer doing?
7. Are you enjoying your coworkers? managers? clients?
8. Are there any particular issues or concerns we can address?
9. What suggestions do you have that could help us improve processes, systems, rules, and procedures?

Your first reaction to the above list of possible questions may be disbelief. You may be wondering if by asking such questions you would be respecting and empowering these employees too much. After all, they are not only your least valued employees, they are also your unmotivated ones. Consider how your view of these suggested questions is implicitly connected with your intentions. By conducting such a questioning interview, is your intention to improve performance, increase motivation, and improve productivity? If so, understanding the system in which they are operating is vitally important.

If, however, you questioned the validity of such questions immediately, you may need to look into the mirror and ask yourself, do you honestly want to retain this employee even if their performance improved?

In adhering to Success Tip #9, "Treat Everyone Completely Honest—Always—Regardless," it is important that you remain completely honest with yourself and with the employee. The above suggested questions are of value for those employees whom you want to retain if performance improves. For those employees whom you have no interest in retaining, it is only fair and appropriate to begin the termination process immediately, strictly adhering to your local employment laws and regulations.

For those employees whom you do wish to improve and retain, if possible, you will notice how the suggested questions are structured. By asking the questions, you reveal that you value this employee. You show interest in their situation. You reveal your desire to understand. You show respect. You show your interest in understanding their particular situation, their particular hardships, and their particular issues. You show that you care about them personally. You reveal that you are interested in their opinions, ideas, and thoughts.

Notice what this suggested list of questions *does not* contain. There is no direct judgment, criticism, or valuation of them as an employee. It also contains no information regarding possible future actions. You remain open to *all* options, including termination, after the interview. You are merely asking questions, gathering information, attempting to understand the situation, so that in the near future you can use the information gathered to address and resolve the situation directly.

During the course of this questioning interview, it is important to pay special attention to their responses. For example, often these employees will speak in future tenses, meaning they may share great stories of excitement of what is to come. They may truly believe the stories they tell and actually anticipate incredible results in the future. It is imperative that you consistently bring future visions into the present and ensure they understand that great visions are built by smaller and more subtle daily activities. These employees may suggest or demand more compensation or greater benefits, often subtly suggesting that their failures are someone else's fault. If at the conclusion of your conversation you feel that the employee has blamed you, the company, or other employees for their lack of production, *be cautious.* Red alert! Such blamers are masters of manipulation, and the blame and finger-pointing will likely continue far into the future. I have invested an enormous amount of time and energy trying to salvage blaming and manipulative employees and have found that the finger-pointing and blaming just gets worse. From personal experience, my suggestion for when dealing with such employees is immediate termination.

To summarize this Success Tip, it is imperative that you recognize, acknowledge, and reward those employees whom you determine to be both highly motivated and highly valued. As we have discussed, this is a high-risk group. They are at risk of leaving to start up their own businesses. They are at risk of being recruited by competing companies. They are at risk of being distracted and discouraged by nonperformers and other less motivated employees. Engaging in a retention system of sharing the wealth is a proven and effective strategy for retaining your Box 1 employees.

Data Collections Manager

I implemented this "share the wealth" program in a creative way with a loyal employee who was one of our first associates. This particular employee joined our company originally as a data compiler. She eventually worked her way up to the position of data collections manager. This involved overseeing all of our data collection efforts, a huge responsibility given that Landvoice was then servicing over 10,000 clients in over seven hundred areas throughout the United States and Canada. She was personally responsible for hiring, firing, training, and quality control for over fifty employees.

By careful observation and asking questions, I knew that she dreamed of taking a cruise to Alaska. She was saving for it. I first became aware of this aspiration by noticing the stunning Alaska photographs on her screen saver. I asked her about the photographs. "No," she said, "I have not been to Alaska, but oh, how I dream of it." After this initial conversation, we discussed it often. On the fifth anniversary of her working with us, we presented her with an all-expense paid cruise to Alaska. She was overwhelmed. It caught the attention of all the other employees as well and became a positive example of what could happen with dedicated and long-term service. It also felt great to share the wealth. She continued as an invaluable and loyal employee for many years. She remains a close and loyal friend.

One warning: Be aware that others in the organization, typically Box 4 employees, may explicitly or implicitly question your apparent favoritism. They may question why, how, and to whom you offer "share the wealth" benefits. When dealing with a divisive situation in which you are accused of favoring one employee over another, Success Tip #9, "Treat Everyone Completely Honest—Always—Regardless," should be your guide. Speak candidly about motivation and value. Speak honestly why and how you value employees differently. Though they may argue against such preferential treatment, they will understand and acknowledge, if not publicly, at least privately, that your employee motivational scale is based on universal characteristics and offers everyone a chance to succeed.

SUCCESS TIP #12
SHARE THE WEALTH!

SUCCESS TIP #13
WHY DIRECT WHEN I CAN DIALOGUE?

Landvoice Accountant Fraud

In 2004, I stepped down as President and CEO of Landvoice to focus on some other outside business interests. My wife, who worked as the accountant in charge of all collections, financial reports, and payment of taxes, hired a replacement as well. I set up a system where I went into the company once a week to correlate with the new president, receive updates on sales and marketing programs, review statistics and financials, and so forth.

I had no reason to believe there were any concerns until one day about a year later I received a disturbing phone call from the IRS. The IRS agent explained that my company had not sent in quarterly tax reports for the past year. "What! There must be a mistake!" I said aloud. She gave me her contact info and suggested I get hold of my accountant and forward her the quarterly reports. I immediately hung up and called my accountant. I relayed the IRS conversation to my accountant.

"Do you know what this is about?" I inquired of the accountant.

My accountant indicated that he had filed the forms and the IRS must have misplaced or misapplied them. He would take care of it.

"Actually, I would like to coordinate this myself," I said. "Please fax the copies of the quarterly reports directly to me."

"No problem," he said. "It'll take me a bit to find them, and I'll get them to you."

The afternoon came and went, and I did not hear back from my accountant. First thing the next morning, I called the accountant again and said impatiently, "Hey, where are those quarterly tax reports?"

"Oh," he said, "I'm sorry. I got busy and forgot. I'll grab them right now."

Three hours later, still no word. I called again, getting more irritated by the minute.

"Where are those quarterly reports?" I demanded angrily. "I want them now!"

He indicated that he had left them at home and was going to get them to me in the morning.

"No. I want them now!" I reiterated. "Run home, grab them, and bring them to me as quickly as possible!"

"OK," he said.

Evening came . . . nothing. I was beside myself when I called the president of the company the next morning and told him what was going on. The president indicated that the accountant was not yet in the office. "When he arrives," I told the president, "bring him into your office, and if he does not have those quarterly reports in hand, fire him on the spot."

I received a call from my president thirty minutes later indicating that my accountant arrived and, when pressed for an explanation, had broken down in tears, confessing that he had not filed those tax returns. He was terminated immediately.

It took external auditors, IRS agents, accountants, attorneys, and the police months to understand and clean up the mess he had left. I ended up paying over $300,000 in outstanding employment taxes and penalties. Further, I learned that he used nearly every possible way in the book to defraud the president, the company, the government, and me. Fake employees were paid wages. Erroneous paid time off was applied. Petty cash was misreported. A myriad of other deceptive accounting techniques totaling tens of thousands of dollars had been employed.

How I wish I had established a culture of dialogue earlier. It would have been simple to assign someone else responsibility to ensure that all state and federal tax forms were reported properly. Such a simple dialogic procedure would have saved hundreds of thousands of dollars and two years of wasted time.

What Is a Culture of Dialogue?

I thoroughly enjoy teaching. I have been teaching business and communication classes at various local colleges and universities for nearly twenty years now. I do not teach, however, in a traditional educational style. I teach employing a dialogic pedagogy. In other words, I teach using dialogue, discussion, and activities, not lectures and tests, as the primary means of learning. The difference is profound.

Have you noticed, after attending a class or meeting, that what you most often remember is not necessarily what the teacher said but, more often, what you said and what you did? This is the foundation on which I suggest you create learning environments at home, school, and business.

Consider how most classrooms—and businesses—are structured. The teacher or manager stands at the front, instructing the students or employees, who typically are seated quietly and expected to listen. If you walk by and look into classrooms and boardrooms across the nation, this is what you typically see. But there is another way. There is a way to structure business and classrooms differently that will yield amazing results.

Have you experienced a classroom where the instructor sat in a circle with the students? Where the opinions of the students, teacher, and text were all equally weighted? Where the traditional hierarchy of the all-knowing teacher standing at the front of the class lecturing the uninformed students from the omnipotent text is dismissed and where everyone participating in the class is equally empowered? Have you experienced a class where your experiences, your thoughts, your stories, and your opinions on the subject not only were heard and appreciated but also created the foundation upon which learning and action occurred? If you have truly experienced one of these rare dialogic experiences, you are lucky indeed. If not, don't be too concerned. Most haven't.

Paulo Freire, a Brazilian-born philosopher and educator, is my teaching mentor. I was introduced to his teaching philosophies while in graduate school. I highly encourage you to read some of his writings and, when possible, experience a learning environment taught from a dialogic perspective. You will be ever grateful for the experience. It may change, as it did for me, the way you structure your home, family, classroom, and business. You can get more information about this teaching and business philosophy on my website, www.brentwarnock.com.

Cultivating a culture of dialogue, in theory, is relatively easy. In your business, family, and classrooms, I suggest that you create and encourage an environment where dialogue, discussion, and participation naturally flow. In a true dialogic environment, open dialogue and discussion are not occasional occurrences; they are the lifeblood of the organization. On the surface, this may not sound like a difficult environment to create. But a real culture of openness and dialogue is actually very rare. Most classrooms and companies simply do not entertain such an ideal. Though many companies may talk the talk, they don't walk the walk.

Obstacles of Creating a Culture of Dialogue

So the question needs to be asked, why aren't more companies, parents, and teachers creating a culture of dialogue? The answer is contained in three simple words: power, authority, and control! From the moment you were born, you have been dependent upon those who have power, authority, and control. You grew up wanting to become big and powerful like your parents, brothers, sisters, grandparents, neighbors, teachers, leaders, business owners, athletic heroes, entertainers, and celebrities. You have been taught from a young age to become independent, mature, and stable. Power, authority, and control are the natural means to these ends. It is, after all, your desire for some combination of power, authority, and control that has created in you an interest in starting and managing a business.

It is understandable that most teachers, business owners, managers, and leaders find it difficult to give up the precious commodities of power, authority, and control that they have worked so hard to obtain. In most cases, they have invested years in dedicated service and schooling. Business owners have risked enormous amounts of time and money in hopes of a return. They earned the present power, authority, and control that they now enjoy. They have sacrificed greatly to be in their present position, so why would anyone freely give up what they have worked so hard to obtain and earn? The key phrase in the prior sentence is "give up." Creating a dialogic culture requires nothing to be given up, but it does necessitate that you share.

Creating an environment where open dialogue is the norm rather than the exception requires that you share power, authority, and control with others. Sharing is nothing more than allowing others to feel, see, experience, and know the same things you do. When you show your willingness to share with others, they will share with you. Consistent with Success Tip #12, "Share the Wealth," sharing is the space where true riches are found. Owners, presidents, managers, teachers, and supervisors who are willing to share power, authority, and control will, ironically, discover that their power and influence is multiplied. You will ultimately become a more effective business owner, teacher, leader, and manager when you create a culture of sharing. You have heard it stated in many ways, but regardless of how it is stated, the message is essentially the same. Only in giving (sharing) do you receive.

Steps to Creating a Culture of Dialogue

There is a five-step process involved in transforming typical authority-based cultures, like classrooms and businesses, into cultures of dialogue. Though I specifically discuss these five steps in terms of how I create a dialogic classroom, you can successfully employ these same steps to set up a dialogue-oriented culture in your professional, business, family, political, coaching, and all other interpersonal realms as well.

First, in order to create an effective culture of dialogue, it is imperative that you allow all the participants in the class or team to get to know each other personally. This means creating a situation where the participants can discuss topics beyond the present business or educational environment. On the first day of class, I ask every member of the group to select another member of the group whom they don't already know. Their objective is to learn enough about each other that each person can effectively introduce the other to the entire class. The class immediately breaks into pairs, and they begin talking. It's fun to hear how the volume of the class increases with each passing moment. At first the discussions are pretty quiet and reserved. They are talking to strangers, and it's understandably a little uncomfortable at first. However, it doesn't take long before the energy in the classroom increases significantly.

It is important that you, as the group facilitator, recognize that this energy increase indicates that the participants are beginning to connect. They are beginning to discover commonalities, make connections, and begin friendships. After six or seven minutes, I ask them to begin wrapping up these conversations. Inevitably, I hear a few groans of disappointment expressed by the participants. They don't want these conversations to end. Every time I do this activity, I am reminded how powerful human interaction really is. Relaxing, comfortable, enjoyable interactions with other humans can be such a positive activity. It's almost like a drug; once you've enjoyed it once, you want it again and again. Yet we so rarely choose to freely engage in interactions, mostly because of fear. In this activity, having an external authority request such interaction seems to dispel much of the fear. Reducing the fear of human interaction is a primary step in effectively creating a dialogic environment.

Once I have regained the group's attention, I surprise the group by asking them to replicate the conversational experience one more time. In other words, I ask them to select a different individual whom they don't know and to converse with this second individual, having the same objective; that is, of getting to know them well enough to introduce them to the group. At the conclusion of this second interview, this dialogic exercise will have taken about fifteen minutes of class time. In terms of benefits, though, these fifteen minutes can yield years of positive results. Why? Because every member of the group now has two friends whom they didn't know just a few minutes before.

The second step in creating a dialogic culture involves creating a space for everyone to speak publicly. This is accomplished by doing group introductions. To start this process, I ask for a volunteer who is willing to briefly introduce one of the individuals whom they interviewed. The length of time you allow for these introductions really depends on the size of your team. In a classroom setting with normally thirty or forty students, I ask that everyone keep their introductions to just a minute or two. In a business setting with fewer participants, the introductions can be longer.

After the first student has briefly introduced one of the other students whom they interviewed, I then ask if the second person who interviewed the same person can fill in with some details. In other words, what did they find out about this person that is different than what was mentioned by the first interviewer? I then give the class a minute to ask any follow-up questions of the student being introduced. Inevitably there are a few additional connections made and questions asked. To continue the introductions, I ask the person who was introduced to tell the group about one of the individuals they interviewed. This natural connective chain of introductions continues until all students have been introduced. I realize such a technique requires an investment in time, but trust me—it is well worth the investment. I have attempted to teach college classes without doing these interviews, and invariably the overall dialogic culture of the class is drastically different.

Obviously, you can create a similar interview and introduction technique in your company or department. Take the first few minutes of every weekly meeting and ask any new employee to talk personally with two existing employees for a few minutes. After these conversations, ask the existing employees to introduce the new employee to the team. But don't stop there. Ensure that you encourage the new employee to likewise share what they learned about their two new associates. These personal conversations will yield great returns. It is important, however, that you encourage individual interviews among the employees rather than simply having the new employee introduce himself or herself publicly to the entire team. Significant interpersonal information and connections will only occur if you encourage personal, face-to-face conversation.

You have likely noticed that when you are asked to introduce yourself to a large group, you remain general and impersonal. In such situations, your intention is to get the attention off of you. Consider the difference, however, if a coworker pulls you to the side and begins asking you questions about yourself in a more personal, private, and relaxed setting. This relational practice creates a safe space in which you share more about you, your family, your accomplishments, and your life than you otherwise would. This information is then shared to the group, not from your own mouth but from others who interviewed you. Not only does the whole team or class learn about you personally, but you now have two individuals with whom you have shared personal information and to whom you naturally feel closer. It's a comfortable way to begin a new job or class.

The third step in creating an effective culture of dialogue is to show that you sincerely care about each individual. I accomplish this by not only personally acknowledging and welcoming them to the next meeting or class, but also more importantly, beginning the next meeting or class by asking the group specific questions regarding each individual who was introduced the last time we met. For example, to start the meeting, I will ask things like "Who used to work at the zoo?" "Who has four brothers?" "Who grew up in Vermont?" "Who knows four programming languages?" And so forth. In a very real way, I am subtly letting all employees or class members know that I value them. That I really listened and cared about them as they were introduced. I reveal that I heard what was being said, that I took notes, and that they were significant to me. It also effectively reminds every individual in the group that everyone in the group is vital and important. It is imperative that the new employee or class member see not only that a different structure of dialogue has been introduced, but also more importantly, that it is practiced.

The fourth step in creating an effective dialogic culture is to introduce to, and then continually remind, the group what a dialogic culture is, how it functions, and what it means. On the second day of class, I always take a moment to clearly introduce the concept of dialogue. We talk openly about what dialogue means and the fact that typical executives, managers, teachers, presidents, parents, and owners run their classrooms, families, and corporations in linear, non-dialogic structures. We mention that most companies and classrooms are structured linearly, meaning that they have typically lecture-oriented, authoritarian, top-down, Boss-knows-best communication styles. I emphasize, however, that this is not how this company or classroom operates. I explain that the culture of this class or office is one of dialogue, participation, communication, sharing, and openness. I explain to the new employees, while simultaneously reminding all the others, that there are no right and no wrong comments. Similarly, there are no right or wrong insights, stories, experiences, suggestions, or proposals. We talk explicitly about how right and wrong, good and bad, and all other value-based judgments are merely word creations and opinions. Undoubtedly, there will be those who claim that their opinions or knowledge is "better" or even "true" because it is based on facts, statistics, or science. It's important, early on, to address such limiting, authoritarian talk directly and quickly when you sense someone is attempting to squelch open conversation by presenting black and white statements of absolute truth. It's relatively easy to do this by simply reminding each participant that facts, statistics, and scientific findings can be, and often are, manipulated to support opposing conclusions. In sum, by verbally emphasizing the safe space that you are interested in creating, you provide a safe conduit in which all opinions, suggestions, and ideas of the group members may flow.

When you implement the two previous steps, your employees will undoubtedly recognize that the culture of your company is inherently different than typical companies. The fifth and most important step of cultivating a culture of dialogue is to practice what you preach. Now that you have introduced how the company is built upon a framework of open and accepting communication, you must ensure that these principles are put in action. All company communications and meetings should be built on the principle of openly asking questions rather than barking out instructions. See Success Tip #6, "Ask Questions," for more informative tips on how to effectively ask questions. It is imperative that you create a culture of equality among all participants. Meetings should not be conducted with you or a manager at the head of table or standing in front of the group. Sit in a circle. Ensure that if a stranger entered into the room, they wouldn't know who the president, manager, or supervisor was. Ensure that you lead by asking questions and allowing space for participation. The most important point is to remain open and nonjudgmental. Ensure that all ideas, suggestions, stories, proposals, and opinions shared by anyone in the group is truly appreciated and not judged. Of course there will be times when a suggestion is made by someone in the group that you have already previously considered, do not agree with, do not understand, or simply need more information in order to seriously consider. In these cases, simply look the participant in the eye, sincerely thank them for their contribution, state directly what your concern or issue is with their suggestion, and then move the discussion forward by asking for any other ideas. It is imperative that you not only listen, respect, and show appreciation for all contributions but also that you constantly remind everyone on the team that there are no bad ideas, wrong opinions, or unimportant comments. When your employees realize they reside in a truly safe place, you will be overwhelmed by a flood of effective new ideas, solutions, and proposals. The result will be astounding. You will have created an environment where everyone feels ownership, everyone feels heard, and everyone feels safe. It sounds like a slice of heaven, doesn't it? It is!

Benefits of a Culture of Dialogue

All of the enormous benefits of creating a culture of dialogue cannot be fully enumerated here. Undoubtedly, you will notice immediate returns in such things as employee morale, quality of creative ideas, teamwork, employee retention, and improved internal and external communication, and the list goes on. However, one of the greatest possible benefits of creating a culture of dialogue is the openness with which all activities of the company now occur. When you as the owner of a company freely share your power, authority, and control with your employees, the winds of change blow far and strong. Everyone notices. When you as the owner, president, or manager asks for suggestions, shows a willingness to really listen nonjudgmentally, and expresses sincere appreciation for any and all suggestions offered, the world literally opens to you. No longer are you limited to ideas from a precious few. Every employee, client, partner, and vendor now becomes a trusted contributor. From this time forth, many of your greatest and most profitable ideas will be generated from the most unlikely sources and in unpredictable ways. In creating a culture of dialogue, you have truly opened the windows, allowing the fresh breeze of success to blow in uninhibited.

Encouraging Other Reviews

One additional benefit of creating a culture of dialogue is worth mentioning. Creating a culture of dialogue inherently leads to the practice of encouraging other reviews. This practice can change mediocre work to superior work, and average effectiveness to excellence. In its simplest form, the notion of encouraging other reviews refers to the policy of having at least two or more people review all work before it is released publicly.

Setting up an "other review" program need not be difficult. The goal is to assign a trusted and independent individual or entity to review all departments and operations of your business. It should be a way of business life that is not only encouraged but also operationally mandated. Every marketing letter, poster, and campaign should have at least two other reviewers before printing. I am sure nearly every business owner has suffered the embarrassment, regret, and financial loss of discovering letters, emails, posters, marketing brochures, or business cards that were designed, printed, and delivered, and only when it was too late did you discover a major mistake. Wasted time, expenses, and resources could be significantly reduced or eliminated altogether if simple other review policies are in place.

In sum, do not be shy about discussing the idea that all marketing, payroll, accounting, and legal materials be reviewed by another employee (a manager, preferably) and, if possible, an external entity *before* distribution. Programmers should be taught the other review policy as well. Talk with programmers openly about how to implement the other review policy so that all design and programming plans are reviewed and discussed by management and outside consultants *prior* to programming.

In summary, ensure that all departments and operations of your business are founded upon an open and honest foundation where questions are freely asked and ideas freely shared. Creating such an open, participatory, and trusted dialogic environment is not as difficult as you may think. It is a natural result of implementing the 13 Critical Success Tips discussed in this book.

SUCCESS TIP #13
CULTIVATE A CULTURE OF DIALOGUE!

SUMMARY OF THE
13 CRITICAL TIPS FOR SUCCESS

1. Fill a Need

2. Engage with Passion

3. Start Simple and Inexpensive

4. Do the Hard Work Yourself—Initially

5. Ensure Systems Are Created, Recorded, and Followed

6. Ask Questions

7. Trust Yourself above All Others—Always

8. Partner with Gatekeepers

9. Treat Everyone Completely Honest—Always—Regardless

10. Be Crystal Clear with Contracts

11. Know the Numbers

12. Share the Wealth

13. Cultivate a Culture of Dialogue

CONCLUSION

THIS BOOK IS AN accumulation of thirty-plus years of research and personal experience. It contains simple, direct, and true accounts of my business successes and failures.

This book provides you with words of experience from one who has gone before—literally, lessons learned through personal experience that will help you traverse a little safer through the rapids of business life. The world of business is dangerous. There are rapids. There are rocks. There are sinkholes and dangers on every side. There are obstacles on the water, in the water, and on the shore that must be avoided.

Yet, despite the dangers, there is no faster, quicker, or more effective way to generate personal wealth than by owning your own business. It works. I stand as a testimonial. I indeed have been richly rewarded because of my involvement in many successful businesses. Most importantly, however, business ownership has allowed me to do what I love.

I know you can do it too! How do I know? I'll repeat a few sentences that I used at the beginning of the book. I am no smarter than you are. I am no different from you. I am just like you. I did it! I was able to retire early. You can too! How do you begin? By implementing the 13 Success Tips discussed in this book. You will be amazed at the results.

I encourage you to begin employing these Success Tips in your life immediately. Start today to pay attention to the needs of others. Get involved in those activities and businesses about which you feel passionate. Start every venture simply and inexpensively. Initially do the hard work yourself so you understand the processes and systems necessary for success. Ask questions of everyone you meet. Trust yourself. Communicate honestly and openly always. Share your wealth and yourself with your employees, partners, and friends. And in all life situations, cultivate a culture of dialogue where open and participative communication permeates all aspects of your life.

I salute you for your willingness to learn from others. The objective of this book was not only to point out the trailheads that lead to success but also to inform you of some of the trails and dangers to be avoided. As I stated in the beginning of this work, experience is a great teacher, but wiser still are those who are humble enough to learn from the experience of others. If the experiences and Success Tips shared in this book help just one individual soar to success, it has been worth the effort.

For more information about Brent Warnock's

* Free Daily Insights

* Free Additional Resources

* Three Fountains Organization

* Additional Books and Articles

Please go to www.brentwarnock.com.

BIBLIOGRAPHY

Emerson, Ralph Waldo. *Essays: First Series* (n.p., 1841).

Geertz, Clifford. *The Interpretation of Cultures* (New York: Basic Books, 1973).

Gerber, Michael E. *The E-myth Revisited: Why Most Small Businesses Don't Work and What to Do about It.* New York: HarperCollins, 2001.

Ginsberg, Steven. "So Many Messages and So Little Time." *Business Outlook*, May 5, 1997.

Hegel, George Wilhelm Friedrich. *Lectures on the Philosophy of History*, trans. J. Sibree (New York: Dover, 1956).

Jakes, T.D. *Reposition Yourself: Living Life without Limits* (New York: Simon & Schuster, 2007).

Reynolds, Siimon, comp. *Thoughts of Chairman Buffett: Thirty Years of Unconventional Wisdom from the Sage of Omaha* (New York: HarperBusiness, 2008).

ABOUT THE AUTHOR

BRENT WARNOCK is a lifelong entrepreneur. He began his business adventures at the age of ten by operating (with his mom as driver) five snack shacks for the local baseball association. After a myriad of business endeavors and enterprises—some successful and some not—Brent was able to fulfill his lifelong dream to retire before the age of forty. He has completed his coursework for a PhD in Communication at the University of Utah and has taught business and communication courses for the past fifteen-plus years at local universities and colleges. He is a popular teacher, speaker, and presenter and founded The Communication Organization (TCO), an organization providing business, communication, and relationship information to an international audience (www.thecommorg.com). In 2003, Brent and his wife, Kathie, were finalists for the Ernst & Young Entrepreneur of the Year award. Brent enjoys weight lifting, golfing, hiking, biking, teaching, and writing. Mostly he enjoys spending time with his three best friends—his children. He resides in Bountiful, Utah.

0 26575 59544 4